A C
Introd
Lotu

ALSO AVAILABLE
(By the same author)

A Concise
Introduction to
Lotus 1-2-3

by

Noel Kantaris

BERNARD BABANI (publishing) LTD.
THE GRAMPIANS
SHEPHERDS BUSH ROAD
LONDON W6 7NF
ENGLAND

PLEASE NOTE

Although every care has been taken with the production of this book to ensure that any projects, designs, modifications and/or programs etc. contained herewith, operate in a correct and safe manner and also that any components specified are normally available in Great Britain, the Publishers and Author(s) do not accept responsibility in any way for the failure (including fault in design) of any project, design, modification or program to work correctly or to cause damage to any equipment that it may be connected to or used in conjunction with, or in respect of any other damage or injury that may be so caused, nor do the Publishers accept responsibility in any way for the failure to obtain specified components.

Notice is also given that if equipment that is still under warranty is modified in any way or used or connected with home-built equipment then that warranty may be void.

First Published - October 1989
Revised Edition - July 1991

British Library Cataloguing in Publication Data:

Kantaris, Noel
        A concise introduction to Lotus 1-2-3
        1. Microcomputer systems. Spreadsheet packages,
        lotus 1-2-3
        I. Title
        005.369

    ISBN 0 85934 206 9

Printed and Bound in Great Britain by Cox & Wyman Ltd, Reading

ABOUT THIS BOOK

This Concise Introduction to Lotus 1-2-3 was written to help the beginner. The book deals mainly with the Lotus 1-2-3 Releases 2.2 & 2.3, but it also covers the earlier Releases 2.0 and 2.01. Users of Release 3.0 and 3.1 could use the book as an introduction to spreadsheet concepts, but must understand that the more advanced ideas of multi-dimensionality, or multi-file display, available in Release 3.0, or windowing, available in Release 3.1, are not covered here.

The material in the book is presented on the "what you need to know first, appears first" basis, although the underlying structure of the book is such that you don't have to start at the beginning and go right through to the end. The more experienced user can start from any section, as the sections have been designed to be self contained.

Lotus 1-2-3 is an integrated package containing three major types of applications; spreadsheets, graphics and data management. The package is operated by selecting commands from menus or by writing special 'macros' which utilise the Lotus Command Language to chain together menu commands. Each method of accessing the package is discussed separately, but the emphasis is mostly in the area of menu-driven command selection.

One of the major enhancements of Release 2.2 & 2.3 over earlier releases of the package is their ability to link files, their ability in minimal recalculation, better graphing (including printing of graphs from within the worksheet), inclusion of undo mode, macro learn mode, search and replace, and an add-in manager. Release 2.2 also supports the Allways spreadsheet publishing add-in allowing for WYSIWYG display, while Release 2.3 manages the same thing with what used to be known as the Impress add-in, which Lotus purchased and incorporated into the package as the Wysiwyg graphical interface, both of which are discussed in this book. In fact, Releases 2.2 & 2.3 provide for all the things users have been wanting for a long time, without the enormous memory requirement of Release 3.0. However, unlike Release 3.0, there is no multi-dimensionality or multi-file display, although Release 2.3 allows for the display of 3D graphs and charts.

This book was written with the busy person in mind. You don't need to read hundreds of pages to find out most there is to know about the subject, when a few pages can do the same thing quite adequately!

ABOUT THE AUTHOR

Graduated in Electrical Engineering at Bristol University and after spending three years in the Electronics Industry in London, took up a Tutorship in Physics at the University of Queensland. Research interests in Ionospheric Physics, lead to the degrees of M.E. in Electronics and Ph.D. in Physics. On return to the UK, he took up a Post-Doctoral Research Fellowship in Radio Physics at the University of Leicester, and in 1973 a Senior Lectureship in Engineering at The Camborne School of Mines, Cornwall, where since 1978 he has also assumed the responsibility of Head of Computing.

ACKNOWLEDGEMENTS

I would like to thank colleagues at the Camborne School of Mines for the helpful tips and suggestions which assisted me in the writing of this book.

TRADEMARKS

Allways is a registered trademark of Funk Software

HP LaserJet is a registered trademark of Hewlett Packard Corporation

IBM, Quietwriter and **PC-DOS** are registered trademarks of International Business Machines Corporation

Intel is a registered trademark of Intel Corporation

Microsoft and **MS-DOS** are registered trademarks of Microsoft Corporation

Lotus 1-2-3 and **Impress** are registered trademarks of Lotus Development Corporation

PostScript is a registered trademark of Adobe Systems, Inc.

CONTENTS

1. INTRODUCTION

Lotus 1-2-3 is a powerful versatile software package which, over the last few years, has proved its usefulness, not only in the business world, but with scientific and engineering users as well. The program's power lies in its ability to emulate everything that can be done by the use of pencil, paper and a calculator. Thus, it is called an 'electronic spreadsheet' or simply a 'spreadsheet', a name also used to describe this and other similar products. Its power is derived from the power of the computer it is running in, and the flexibility and accuracy with which it can deal with the solution of the various applications it has been programmed to manage. These can vary from budgeting to forecasting to the solution of scientific and engineering problems.

Lotus 1-2-3 comes in several flavours; Version 2.x (the subject of this book), incorporating Release 2.0, 2.01, 2.2 and 2.3, running mainly on IBM XTs and compatibles (computers equipped with Intel's 8086 or 8088 processor). Then, there is Version 3.x (the subject of another, more advanced book) encompassing Releases 3.0 and 3.1 which require a more powerful computer as a platform, such as an IBM AT, PS/2 or compatible (a computer equipped with Intel's superior 80286, 80386 or 80486 processor). Versions 3.x make use of certain programmable aspects of the 80286 and 80386 processors and, therefore, cannot run on computers with the less powerful processors, but there is nothing to stop you from running any of the versions 2.x on any IBM compatible computer, irrespective of the type of processor. All the above versions run under the DOS operating system, while the latest version of the program, 1-2-3/W, requires the advanced processing power of computers equipped with at least the 286 processor, running under DOS, but with the Windows front-end graphical interface. Last but not least, there is Lotus 1-2-3/G, the Presentation Manager version, using a graphical interface front-end, but running under the OS/2 operating system.

This book deals with Lotus 1-2-3 Version 2.x. As releases within this version are downward compatible, Release 2.2 & 2.3 will be used as the main platform for discussion, but variations between them and earlier releases of the package will be pointed out whenever they occur.

Release 2.2 & 2.3 Features

In general, it is worth upgrading to either Release 2.2 or Release 2.3, which offer several options not found in earlier releases. These are:

Undo
Search and Replace
Minimal recalculation
Set the width of a range of columns
Linking files on disc
Printer settings sheet
PostScript laser output support
Graphs settings sheet
Improved graph appearance
Quickgraph for groups of data
Built-in Manager access from main menus
WYSIWYG display & spreadsheet publishing
Print text and graphics on the same page
Learn mode for macros with 11 new macro commands
Macro run key with unlimited macro names
Macro library manager
Macro debugging step mode
Menu macro commands
Server and Node packs
Network file locking
Network printing
Support for IBM, NOVELL and 3COM networks.

In addition to the above new features, Release 2.3 also offers:

New graph types, including 3D effects
Background printing & ability of to save printer information
Mouse support, dialogue boxes and preselection of ranges
Context sensitive help system
Ability to view the contents of files on disc.

Releases 2.2 & 2.3 allow you to improve the overall looks of your charts and reports, the very medium used to communicate information to others. The former is achieved through substantial changes and improvements to the charting and graphing capabilities of the package, while the latter is achieved with either the help of the Allways spreadsheet add-in, in the case of Release 2.2, or the Wysiwyg module in the case of Release 2.3, which are supplied with the package. These allow you complete formatting control over the appearance of your reports, with the capability of producing professional-looking business forms or financial reports which can include both numerical and graphical information on the same page. Both the Allways and the Wysiwyg graphical interfaces will be discused in this book.

Installing 1-2-3

It is assumed here that for releases earlier than Release 2.2 of Lotus 1-2-3, you have followed the instructions accompanying the software, relating to its installation on the hard disc of your computer, or its installation and use from a floppy drive. If you are installing Release 2.3, then skip the next section because unlike Release 2.2 which requires you to run three separate install programs and know something of DOS, Release 2.3 accomplishes installation by running a single install program.

Installing Release 2.2:

To install Release 2.2, make sure that the very first thing you do is put the System disc in the A: drive, type A: to log onto it, then type

    init

and press the <Enter> key. You will then be asked to type in your name and your company's name. Having done this, then and only then, log onto the C: drive by typing C:, and type

    md\lot123v2

or a subdirectory of your choice and press <Enter>, then log onto it by typing

    cd\lot123v2

press the <Enter> key, and type

    copy a:*.*

and press <Enter>. This transfers all the files from the floppy disc in the A: drive to the subdirectory in the C: drive. Repeat this last command while each of the Lotus 1-2-3 discs (not the

Allways discs) is inserted in the A: drive. After you have completed this task, type

   install

and press the <Enter> key. At this stage, Lotus 1-2-3 displays a 'Main Menu', as follows:

   First-Time Installation
   Change Selected Equipment
   Advanced Options
   Exit Install Program

from which you should choose the 'First-Time Installation' option which provides you with step-by-step instructions for completing the installation procedure. It is here that you specify the type of screen, printer and so on. At a later stage, you can return to the 'Install' program from the "1-2-3 Access System" to change the selected equipment or select the advanced options.

Release 2.2 requires you to set-up the Allways add-in before you can use the spreadsheet publishing facility of the package, but you will need to have a hard-disc system with approximately 1.1MB of free space, plus at least 512K of conventional memory. If you do not have sufficient space on your hard disc, you could omit installing Allways, but you could not improve the looks of your displayed or printed work.

To install Allways, insert the Allways Setup Disc in the A: drive and type A: to log onto it, then type

   awsetup

and press <Enter>. The Allways displays the 'Setup' main menu from which you should choose the 'First-Time Setup' option. It is here that Allways lets you specify what type of equipment you are using, then it transfers all appropriate files from the various floppy discs onto your hard disc.

Installing Release 2.3:
To install Release 2.3, insert the 'Install' disc in the A: drive, type A: to log onto it, then type

   install

and press the <Enter> key. Lotus 1-2-3 will display a screen in which you are asked to enter your name and your company's

4

name, after which you are presented with the 'Install' screen. Pressing <Enter> causes another screen to be displayed which informs you which files, corresponding to the listed programs, will be transferred on to your hard disc, if you continue.

At this point, you are asked whether you would like the programs to be transferred on to the C:\123R23 subdirectory. Being a matter of preference, we have chosen to change this to C:\lot123v2. On pressing <Enter> the installation program creates the named subdirectory and transfers automatically the appropriate files to it, provided there is enough space on your hard disc. After all the files have been copied, the program displays a screen headed with the message 'File Transfer Successful' and informs you that the next step is to specify your equipment.

Next, Lotus 1-2-3 displays the 'Main Menu' from which you should choose the 'Select Your Equipment' option, which provides you with step-by-step instructions for completing the installation procedure. It is here that you specify the type of screen adaptor, printer, etc. At a later stage you can return to the 'Install' program from the "1-2-3 Access System" to change the selected equipment or specify Wysiwyg option. For the present, proceed with the installation of the fonts (for use with Wysiwyg), by selecting the 'Basic' option. After a short time, the program displays the 'successful installation' message.

Upgrading Other 1-2-3 Add-In Programs:
Most Release 2.0 & 2.01 add-in programs will work with Releases 2.2 & 2.3. However, some programs were not developed using the Lotus Developer Tools and, if that is the case, will not work correctly with Releases 2.2 & 2.3. If you have difficulty in running any of your add-in programs, contact the original manufacturer for a possible upgrade to run with Release 2.2 or 2.3.

Before you can use a Release 2.0 or 2.01 add-in program with Release 2.2 or 2.3, you must repeat the installation instructions that came with the add-in program. If such an add-in program installs a copy of the 'Add-In Manager' in your 1-2-3 set, you should remove it as it can save up to 21K of memory. To remove the 'Add-In Manager' from the 1-2-3 driver set, log onto the subdirectory containing your Release 2.2 or 2.3 program by typing **cd\lot123v2** (if that is its name), and type del_mgr 123.set

if you have allowed the program to use the filename **123.set** for your driver set. Otherwise use the name you gave it.

Loading the 1-2-3 Program

If your are using an already installed package on hard disc, then it is most likely that the files which make up the complete package will be found in a sub-directory of your computer's hard disc, and that the actual program can be invoked by typing **Lotus** or **123** at the root directory's prompt. An appropriately written batch file would then locate the sub-directory in which the program's files reside and load the "1-2-3 Access System" into memory.

If you have just installed the package in your computer's hard disc and in the suggested subdirectory, then use the **edlin** or a similar editor to produce an appropriate batch file, call it **lotus.bat**, which could contain the following commands:

```
@echo off
cls
cd\lot123v2
lotus
cd\
```

If your system is correctly implemented, typing **lotus** should display the "1-2-3 Access System" menu, as follows:

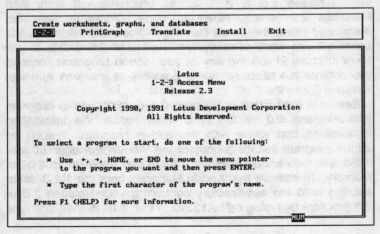

The second line of the "1-2-3 Access System" menu displays the options available to you, while the top line is the description line of the highlighted option. It describes what will happen if the highlighted option is selected. In the case of Release 2.2, this is the other way round; the top line displays the Lotus menu while the second line is the description line.

Note that to start with, the "1-2-3" option is highlighted and that the highlighted bar can be moved by pressing the <Right> arrow, <Left> arrow or <Spacebar> (the latter might not work with the older releases of the program). As the highlighted bar moves, the description line changes. Selection of an option can also be made by typing the first character of an option given in the menu. Previous releases of the program, include an additional 'View' option in the "1-2-3 Access System" menu which allows the user to choose between three options; an 'Introduction' to the worksheet, graphs, and database, 'A Sample Session' in which you evaluate alternative business strategies, and 'New Features in Release 2'.

Release 2.3 includes a new online tutorial to learning 1-2-3 and Wysiwyg. The appropriate programs are called 1-2-3-Go! and Wysiwyg-Go!, respectively. These tutorials can either be started from DOS (for less experience users), by changing to the 1-2-3 program directory and typing **learn123** or **learnwiz**, depending on your learning needs, or (for more experienced users) from a 1-2-3 worksheet, by selecting the /**Add-In Attach** command (more about command selection later), then choose the TUTOR.ADN, select the key you would like to start 1-2-3-Go!, choose **Invoke**, and select TUTOR. As you can see, the latter method requires you to know your way around 1-2-3, before you can invoke the tutorials to learn how to do it!

Loading the "1-2-3 Access System" menu takes up some of your computer's memory because it remains resident. You can start 1-2-3 or any of its utilities by typing **123** (to load 1-2-3), **pgraph** (to load PrintGraph), **install** (to load Install), or **trans** (to load Translate) while logged in the Lotus 1-2-3 subdirectory, or by writing appropriate batch files.

Finally, Lotus 1-2-3 only supports code page 437. So if you have set your computer to any other code page (refer to your DOS documentation if you are unsure by what is meant by code page), you must edit your **autoexec.bat** file appropriately.

Running 1-2-3:

To load the 1-2-3 program, highlight the first option on the "1-2-3 Access System" menu and press the <Enter> key. This will load the relevant program into your computer's memory, after first displaying for a short time the Lotus licence notice. When the program is loaded, a blank worksheet, with a distinctive border, is displayed on the screen as shown below:

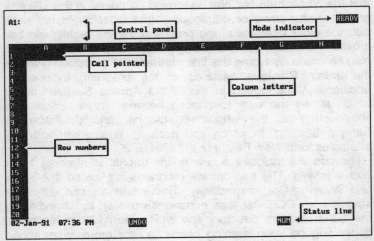

Lotus 1-2-3 sets up a huge electronic page, or spreadsheet, in your computer's memory, many times larger than the small part shown on your screen. The location of the highlighted bar of the cell pointer is constantly monitored by the 'cell indicator' which is to be found on the top left-hand corner of the screen. As the highlighted bar moves, this indicator displays the address of the cell.

Your screen is divided into several areas; the area within which you can move the highlighted bar is referred to as the working area, while the letters and numbers in the highlighted border form the reference points. The highlighted bar cannot be moved into these border areas. If you try it, the speaker bleeps.

Finally, the very top and bottom lines of the screen are reserved for displaying certain 'control information'. For example, on the very top right-hand corner of the screen, the 'mode indicator' displays the word READY in inverse video and, if you are using a recent release of Lotus 1-2-3, the date and time appears on the last line of the screen. Releases 2.2 & 2.3 also displays the word UNDO to the right of the date and time. For a list of both 'mode' and 'status' indicators, refer to Appendix A.

In the case of Release 2.3, the screen has five icons at the extreme right-hand side of the display, under the READY mode indicator. You can use the mouse to point to and click (by pressing the left mouse button) at any of these icons to move the highlighted bar left, right, up or down. Clicking on the question mark (?) displays a help screen as shown below. Note that clicking on the question mark causes the mode indicator to change from READY to HELP.

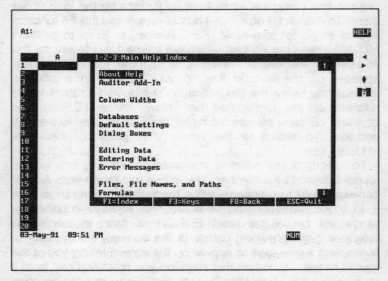

Worksheet Navigation

Navigation around the spreadsheet is achieved by use of the four arrow cursor keys. Each time one of these keys is pressed, the highlighted bar moves one position right, down, left or up, depending on which arrow key was pressed. The <PgDn> and <PgUp> keys can also be used to move vertically 20 rows at a time. A spreadsheet can be thought of as a two-dimensional table made up of rows and columns. The point where a row and column intersect is called a cell.

9

When you have finished navigating around the spreadsheet, press the <Home> key which will bring you to the Home cell position, (A1), which is the top left-hand corner of the spreadsheet. Individual cells are identified by column and row location (in that order), with present size extending to 256 columns and 8192 rows. The columns are labelled from A to Z, followed by AA to AZ, HA to BE, and so on, to IV, while the rows are numbered from 1 to 8192. The reference points of a cell are known as the cell address.

The GOTO Command:
Sometimes it is necessary to move to a specific address in the spreadsheet which, however, is too far from our present position that using the arrow keys might take far too long to get there. To this end, Lotus 1-2-3 has implemented the **F5** function key as a 'go to' command. For example, to jump to position HZ5000, press the **F5** key, which will cause 1-2-3 to ask for the address of the cell to which it is to jump to. This request appears on the second line on your screen, in a position immediately below the cell indicator. The default address is the address of the highlighted bar. Now, typing HZ5000 and pressing <Enter>, causes the highlighted bar to jump to that cell address. To return to the Home (A1) position, press the <Home> key.

To specify a cell address you must always key one or two letters followed by a number. The letters can range from A to IV corresponding to a column, while the numbers can range from 1 to 8192 corresponding to a row. An address outside this range will cause the word ERROR to flash in the 'mode indicator' (top right-hand corner of the screen), the speaker to bleep, and a message to appear on the screen telling you of the invalid range. To correct this situation you must first exit from it by pressing the <Esc> key. In fact, the <Esc> key can be used to cancel a command and escape from a situation before an error occurs.

Entering Basic Information
We will now investigate how information can be entered into a worksheet. But first, return to the Home (A1) position by pressing the <Home> key, then type the words:

PROJECT ANALYSIS

As you type, the characters appear in the control area of the worksheet under the cell indicator. If you make a mistake, press the <BkSp> key to erase the previous letter or the <Esc> key to start again. When you have finished, press <Enter>.

Note that what you have typed now appears in cell A1, even though part of the word ANALYSIS appears to be in cell B1. Thus, typing any letter at the beginning of a cell entry causes 1-2-3 to accept the entry as a 'label', automatically preceding it with the apostrophe (') character. Pressing <Enter> inserts the information as a 'label' into the highlighted cell. If the length of a label is longer than the width of a cell, it will continue into the next cell, provided that cell is empty, otherwise the label will be truncated. Now move the highlighted bar to cell B3, type

    Jan

and press <Enter>. Use the <Right> arrow key to move to the next cell (C3), type

    Feb

and this time press the <Right> arrow key. The arrow keys can be used to both enter information into a cell and move to the next cell. Now move to cell A4, type

    \=

and press <Enter>. Note that typing the backslash (\) and then following it with any character it replicates that character and fills the entire cell with it. Repeat this last entry in cells B4 and C4 so that a double line appears, extending the full width of cells A4..C4. Finally, move the cell pointer to A5 and type

    Consult:

then, enter the numbers 14000 and 15000 in cells B5 and C5. What you should have on your screen now is the following:

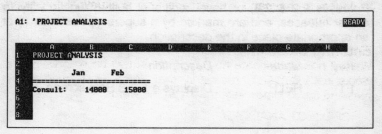

Note how the labels 'Jan' and 'Feb' do not appear above the numbers 14000 and 15000. This is because by default, labels are left justified, while numbers are right justified.

The EDIT Command:
One way of correcting the looks of this spreadsheet is to also right-justify the labels 'Jan' and 'Feb' within their respective cells. To do this, move the cell pointer to B3 and press the **F2** function key which changes the mode indicator to EDIT and allows you to edit the contents of the cell. The cursor is now moved into the control area below the cell indicator. What you see is:

B3: 'Jan

with the cursor at the end of the label. Use the <Left> arrow key to move the cursor under the apostrophe (') and delete it with the <Del> key. Then type the double quote (") character which will be inserted to take the place of the deleted apostrophe. On pressing the <Enter> key, the label is now right justified within its cell and the mode indicator changes back to READY.

To cancel any changes made to the worksheet since 1-2-3 was last in READY mode, press the **Alt+F4** key-stroke (hold the **Alt** key down and while holding it down, press the **F4** function key). Pressing again the **Alt+F4** key-stroke, restores the changes. The UNDO mode is only available in Releases 2.2 & 2.3.

Using Function Keys
Each function key, with the exception of **F6**, performs two operations; one when pressed by itself, and another when pressed while the **Alt** key is held down.

The function keys, together with what they do when pressed, are listed in the table which follows. Six of these are new to Releases 2.2 & 2.3, or have additional built-in functionality to earlier releases, and are marked by a superscript asterisk (*) at an appropriate place in the description.

Key	Mode	Description
F1	HELP	Displays a 1-2-3 Help screen.

F2	EDIT	Enters EDIT mode and displays the current cell contents in the control panel.
F3	NAME	Displays a full screen of filenames when in FILES mode, or a menu of range names when in POINT mode. *When entering a formula, pressing **F3** after an arithmetic operator or a parenthesis displays a list of range names which can then be included in the formula.
F4	ABS	Toggles a cell or a range of cells between relative, absolute, and mixed addressing.
F5	GOTO	Moves the cell pointer to a specified location.
F6	WINDOW	Moves cell pointer between two windows. *When in MENU mode, press **F6** to toggle the display of setting sheets between on/off.
F7	QUERY	Repeats most recent /**Data, Query** operation.
F8	TABLE	Repeats most recent /**Data, Table** operation.
F9	CALC	Recalculates all formulae (READY mode only). Converts formula to its value (VALUE and EDIT modes).
F10	GRAPH	Draws a graph using the current graph settings.
Alt+F1	COMPOSE	When used with alphanumeric keys, creates characters you cannot enter directly from the keyboard.
Alt+F2	STEP	Allows macro execution one step at a time, which facilitates debugging.
Alt+F3	RUN	*Allows selection of a macro name from a display of named worksheet ranges. Pressing <Esc> switches to POINT mode so you can highlight the range containing the macro instructions you want to run.

Alt+F4	UNDO	*Cancels any changes made to the worksheet since 1-2-3 was last in READY mode. Press again to restore the changes.
Alt+F5	LEARN	*Turns LEARN mode on and records key-strokes. Press again to turn off the feature.
Alt+F7	APP1	*Activates add-in program assigned to key, if any.
Alt+F8	APP2	*Activates add-in program assigned to key, if any.
Alt+F9	APP3	*Activates add-in program assigned to key, if any.
Alt+F10	APP4	Displays add-in menu, if key has not been assigned to an add-in program. *Otherwise, it activates the add-in program assigned to the key.

The detailed use of these function keys will be discussed as and when needed. Other function key strokes which are used from within Allways, will be listed and explained separately when the Allways program is introduced.

It is worth noting that should you need help, at any stage, pressing the function key **F1** will produce the required effect. The first help screen, when the mode indicator is on READY, is a 1-2-3 Help Index. Try it now. Any topic can be selected from the displayed list on your screen by simply moving the highlighted bar to the require choice and pressing the <Enter> key. Furthermore, the help command is context sensitive which means that pressing the **F1** function key while in a particular mode, or in the middle of entering a command, brings up the help screens relevant to the mode you are in, or the command being entered.

The File Commands

To activate the menu system provided by 1-2-3, press the front slash key (/) which is found on the query (?) key. The forward slash (/) must not be confused with the back slash (\) which has a totally different meaning.

On pressing /, a horizontal menu in the 'Lotus' style appears on the second line of the screen, as shown on the next page.

The line below the menu describes the option that is currently highlighted by the bar. This menu operates in the same manner as the menu we came across when we first loaded the "1-2-3 Access System".

The highlighted bar can be moved by using the <Right> or <Left> arrows, the <Home> key or the <Spacebar>. Note that the 'mode indicator' at the top right-hand corner of the screen now reads MENU.

To make a menu selection, say **F** (for File), we can either highlight the option and press <Enter>, or simply press the first letter of the command (**F** in this case). We shall use this last method to select 'File' - indeed, from now on, we will always use the first letter method as it is quicker. If you make a mistake, simply press the <Esc> key and try again. On selection of 'File', the mode indicator on the top right-hand corner of the screen changes to FILES and a sub-menu of options appears on the screen.

Saving a Worksheet:
Now, let us assume that we would like to stop at this point, but would like to save the work entered so far, before leaving the program. First, let us return to the Home position by pressing the <Home> key, then press

/	to reveal the menus
F	to select **File**
S	to select **Save**.

On pressing **S** (for Save), 1-2-3 asks you to name a file into which your work is to be saved. The message appears on the second line of your screen, and the default sub-directory to which such data files will be saved is also displayed. This should be preferably the c:\lot123v2\data subdirectory. Having a separate subdirectory for your data, makes it easier to manage both package updates and data back-ups.

The *.wk1 at the end of the second line of the display, indicates the type of files listed in the line below. These are shown in the following two screens as FILE1.WK1 and FILE2.WK1 which perhaps contain someone else's work.

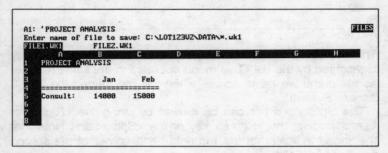

The above screen is what you get with Release 2.2, while the screen below is the corresponding one for Release 2.3. The latter has an additional first line with appropriate icons for making selection of files easier with the use of the mouse.

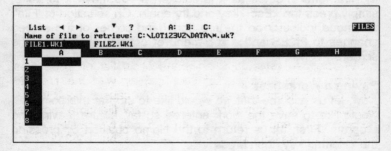

If you are the first person to be using the package, it is more likely that there will not be any filenames of previously saved work. If this is not the case with the data path, and you still want to save your files on your hard disc, it is imperative to change the default data file path (see next section), so as to save the files you create into a separate directory from that in which Lotus 1-2-3 program files are kept.

To save the present contents of memory to a file you must either highlight an existing filename with the help of the cursor keys or type a new filename. If you choose to save your work under an existing filename, you will be asked whether you would like the contents of the file on disc to be 'Replaced' by the contents of the current memory. If you do, type **R** to confirm your decision. If, on the other hand, you choose to save your work under a new filename, then the moment you start typing its name, the menu of existing filenames disappears and what you type replaces the *.wk1 at the end of the data path. To end this session, type

    PROJECT1

and press the <Enter> key.

The name of the file can be composed of a mixture of letters and numbers, but must not be longer than 8 characters. The extension .WK1 will be added automatically by the program.

Summarising:- To save worksheet files, first, make sure that the mode indicator is on READY. If not, press the <Esc> key as many times as necessary to achieve it, then press

/	to reveal the menus
F	to select **File**
S	to select **Save**.

Lotus 1-2-3 asks for a filename to save under. If your current work has not been saved before, and there are other data files in the specified drive\path, an alphabetical list of these files appears on the third line of your display with the first file highlighted. Selecting an existing filename causes 1-2-3 to ask for replacement confirmation. Typing a new filename replaces the *wk1 at the end of the data path. You can type a filename in either lower-case letters or uppercase letters, but 1-2-3 displays filenames in uppercase letters only.

If, you have just edited a previously saved worksheet and you want to save your work again, on selecting **Save**, the previously specified name is offered as a default filename. Pressing <Enter> causes 1-2-3 to ask for confirmation. If, on the other hand, you would like to edit the default filename, then you must first press the space-bar (which adds a space at the end of the existing filename) before you can use the cursor keys, <BkSp>

key, or <Del> key. However, before beginning to edit the default drive\path\filename, use the <BkSp> key to remove the added space, otherwise 1-2-3 will not accept your efforts as a valid filename. You <u>must</u> delete the added space.

Changing the Default Data Drive/Path:
Assuming you want to change the default drive/path to which your data is to be saved, do the following:

First, make sure that the mode indicator is on READY. If not, press the <Esc> key as many times as necessary to achieve it, then press

/	to reveal the menus
W	to select **Worksheet**
G	to select **Global**
D	to select **Default**
D	to select **Directory**

On the second line, the current directory for data is displayed. To change this to, say, the A: drive, type A:.

If, on the other hand you wanted to save your work on the C: drive, then provided a \data sub-directory to the main 1-2-3 directory already exists, type c:\lot123v2\data.

If you want to make this change permanent, then press

| **U** | to select **Update** |

From now on data will be saved and retrieved from the newly 'Updated' drive\path. Finally, press the <Esc> key to return to the READY mode. Each time <Esc> is pressed, 1-2-3 returns to the previous sub-menu. Repeating the process will eventually return you to the READY mode.

Retrieving a Worksheet:
An already saved worksheet file can be retrieved by pressing

/	to reveal the menus
F	to select **File**
R	to select **Retrieve**.

Lotus 1-2-3 asks for a filename to load. The first data file saved in the specified drive\path is highlighted. Pressing <Enter>, retrieves the highlighted file or pressing the <Right> arrow cursor key highlights the next file. Pressing NAME (**F3**) displays filenames in full screen mode. When a file is loaded in memory in this manner it replaces what was currently held there. Therefore, you don't have to erase the memory before retrieving a new worksheet.

Since you will be working with a lot of different files, it is useful to know which file is loaded in memory at any given time. Lotus allows you to replace the Date & Time indicator with the Filename indicator. To do this, type the following commands from the READY mode

/	to reveal the menus
W	to select **Worksheet**
G	to select **Global**
D	to select **Default**
O	to select **Other**
C	to select **Clock**
F	to select **Filename**

If you want to make this change permanent, then press

U	to select **Update**
Q	to select **Quit**

From now on the filename of the retrieved file will appear at the bottom left of your display in place of the Date & Time indicator.

Lotus 1-2-3 provides a facility whereby files can be merged in various ways. This facility can be reached from the READY mode by pressing

/	to reveal the menus
F	to select **File**
C	to select **Combine**

which reveals a sub-menu with **Copy**, **Add** & **Subtract** options.

The Undo Feature

A very useful feature Lotus have added to their 1-2-3 Release 2.2 & 2.3 packages is the ability to cancel the most recent operations that have changed your worksheet data and/or settings. Pressing the UNDO key (Alt+**F4**), causes 1-2-3 to automatically restore worksheet data or settings which existed the last time 1-2-3 was in READY mode. In addition, if you use the UNDO feature and then change your mind, pressing UNDO again, restores your work to the latest changes.

By default, the first time you use 1-2-3, the UNDO feature is on in the case of Release 2.2 and off in the case of Release 2.3. It is easy to tell if this is so, by looking for the UNDO indicator on the status line at the bottom of your screen which, however, only appears after a file has been retrieved into memory. If the UNDO indicator is not displayed, first erase the current worksheet from memory (see beginning of next chapter on how to do this), then enable it by pressing

/	to reveal the menus
W	to select **Worksheet**
G	to select **Global**
D	to select **Default**
O	to select **Other**
U	to select **Undo**
E	to select **Enable**
U	to select **Update**

If you attempt to issue the above commands while a worksheet is in memory, 1-2-3 will tell you that it cannot enable the undo feature, because the memory it requires to do so is otherwise in use.

Because the UNDO facility creates a temporary back-up copy of all the data and settings affected by the current operation, it uses computer memory that may otherwise be needed to run the program. Unless your computer is fitted with a large amount of RAM, you may find you have to disable UNDO frequently, especially if you work with large macros or spreadsheets.

Quitting 1-2-3

To quit the program, make sure that 1-2-3 is in READY mode. If it is not, press the <Esc> key as many times as it is necessary for the mode indicator to change to READY, then press

| / | to reveal the menus |
| Q | to select **Quit** |

which asks for confirmation, because if you quit a session without saving your worksheet you will lose any changes made. Pressing **Y** (for Yes) ends the 1-2-3 session.

2. FILLING IN A WORKSHEET

We will use, as an example on how a worksheet can be built up, the few entries on 'Project Analysis' which we used in the Introduction to Lotus 1-2-3. If you haven't saved the PROJECT1 example, don't worry as you could just as easily start afresh. However, if you have a worksheet with unwanted entries in it, clear it from memory (see below) before you start creating a new worksheet.

Erasing a Worksheet:
To erase a worksheet from memory, which also clears the screen (make sure you have saved your work first), press

/	to reveal the menus
W	to select **Worksheet**
E	to select **Erase**
Y	for 'Yes', to confirm command.

Always use this command to clear memory and screen of unwanted information before starting with a new worksheet. Never switch off your computer in order to clear its memory of unwanted work! Computers are best left running for the entire working period, as switching them on and off too many times in a day can cause hardware failure.

Editing a Worksheet
If you have saved PROJECT1, then enter 1-2-3 and at the READY mode, press

/	to reveal the menus
F	to select **File**
R	to select **Retrieve**.

If there are a lot of files with the .WK1 extension on disc, you could force their display on more than one line, by pressing the **F3** function key.

Next, highlight PROJECT1 and press <Enter> to display the worksheet on screen. Then, use the **F2** function key to 'Edit' existing entries or simply re-type the contents of cells so that you end up with the worksheet shown overleaf.

```
        A          B         C         D         E         F         G         H
1  PROJECT ANALYSIS: ADEPT CONSULTANTS LTD
2
3                  Jan       Feb       Mar     1st Quart
4  =========================================================
5  Consult:       14000     15000     16000     45000
6  =========================================================
7  Costs:
8  Wages           2000      3000      4000
9  Travel           400       500       600
10 Rent             300       300       300
11 Heat/Lght        150       200       150
12 Phone/Fax        250       300       350
13 Adverts         1100      1200      1300
14  --------------------------------------------------------
15 Tot Cost:
16 =========================================================
17 Profit:
18 =========================================================
19 Cumulat:
20 =========================================================
PROJECT1.WK1                    UNDO                        NUM
```

Label Prefixes:

Label prefixes allow you to control the way labels are aligned within their cell. The five available label prefixes are:

Prefix	Purpose
'	(apostrophe) is used to left justify the label within a cell
"	(quotation marks) is used to right justify a label within a cell
^	(caret) is used to centre a label within a cell
\	(backslash) is used to fill a cell with the repeated character(s) that follow it
|	(appears as a split vertical bar on the keyboard) is used to embed set-up strings. If it is located at the beginning of a row, the data in that row will not be printed. If it is located anywhere else in a row, the data in that row is printed. To print the actual split vertical line (|), prefix it with an apostrophe (').

With these in mind, the information in cell A1 (PROJECT ANALYSIS: ADEPT CONSULTANTS LTD) was entered left justified. In fact, we just typed in the label in A1 without preceding it with the apostrophe. Similarly, all the labels appearing in column A were just typed in as shown. This is the default entry mode for labels, with 1-2-3 automatically adding the apostrophe.

If you have several rows or columns of labels whose alignment you would like to change, move the cell pointer to the beginning of the relevant row or column, and press

/	to reveal the menus
R	to select **Range**
L	to select **Label**

select one of the displayed options, **Left, Right** or **Centre**, then move the cell pointer in the required direction to highlight the whole range containing the labels whose alignment you want to change, and press <Enter>.

The labels relating to the months in cells B3, C3, D3 and E3 were centre justified within their respective cell. Note that had we attempted to just type

   1st Quart

in cell E3, on pressing <Enter> 1-2-3 would have bleeped and refused to accept the information into the cell. This is because the label starts with the numeral 1 which causes 1-2-3 to expect a number. However, what follows is not a number, therefore the objection.

Repeated information, like the double line stretching from A4 to E4 was entered by first highlighting cell A4 and typing

   \=

On pressing <Enter> the equals (=) character fills the entire cell.

The /Copy Command:

To replicate information into other cells we could repeat the above procedure (in this particular case entering the \= characters) within each cell, or we could use the **/C** (for Copy) command which is by far the quickest and easiest method of copying information from one cell (or a range of cells) to a range of other cells. This command is not restricted only to repeated character-type information, but can equally well be used with numbers or formulae. When copying a formula in this way, references to cells within the formula are adjusted relative to their new position.

To copy the contents of cell A4 to the cell range B4 through E4, ensure that you are in the READY mode (press <Esc> until you are), then move the cell pointer to A4, and press

/   to reveal the menus
C   to select **Copy**.

At this point, you'll be asked for the range to copy from. In this case, the cell pointer (note that the mode indicator has changed to POINT) is at the cell we want to start copying from and the entire copy range is highlighted (i.e. the range is given by A4 to A4), therefore press

<Enter>   to confirm the range

which will cause 1-2-3 to ask you to enter the range to copy to. Now press

<Right>   to move to the starting location of the range
<.>   (period) to anchor the first target cell
<Right>   to select and highlight target cell range
<Enter>   to confirm target range.

If you make any mistakes and copy information into cells you did not mean to, then use the **E** (for Erase) command, as discussed below.

The /Range Erase Command:
To erase a range, or block of adjacent cells, highlight the first cell of the range or one corner cell of the block, and press

/   to reveal the menus
R   to select **Range**
E   to select **Erase**

then press the <Right>, <Left>, <Up> or <Down> arrow keys as many times as needed to highlight the range of cells, or block of cells, you want to erase, and press

<Enter>   to confirm range or block selection.

If you make a mistake in highlighting the wrong starting cell of a range of cells or a block of cells, press <Esc> to release the automatic anchorage, use the arrow keys to move to the required cell, press <.> (period) to anchor the newly selected cell, and carry on as before.

Entering Numbers and Formulae:

When numbers are entered into a cell, or reference is made to the contents of a cell by preceding the cell address with an arithmetic operator, or a Lotus 1-2-3 function (which is preceded by the @ sign) is entered into a cell, then the mode indicator changes from READY to VALUE.

Returning to our example of PROJECT ANALYSIS, move the cell pointer to B5 and start entering the 'consultancy' income of the company. As soon as the first number is typed into the line below the cell indicator (the number 1 of the 14000), the mode indicator changes to VALUE and when the complete amount is typed in, pressing <Enter> inserts it into the specified cell, right justifying the number within the cell width. Now complete typing in the rest of the amounts into cells C5 and D5.

We can find the 1st quarter total income from consultancy, by highlighting cell E5 and typing

   +B5+C5+D5

and on pressing <Enter> the total first quarter consultancy income is added from the above formula and the result placed in cell E5. Notice that the above formula is preceded by a plus (+) sign. Had we not typed this first '+' sign into the formula, 1-2-3 would have mistaken the formula for a label and no calculation would have resulted.

Now complete the insertion into the worksheet of the various amounts under 'costs' and then save the result into the file PROJECT2 before going on any further. Remember that saving your work on disc often enough is a good thing to get used to, as even the shortest power cut can cause the loss of hours of hard work!

Order of Precedence in Formulae:

The table shown on the next page, lists the arithmetic, logical, and string operators available in 1-2-3, with their associated order of precedence. What we mean by precedence is the priority order in which 1-2-3 evaluates a formula. The lower the priority number, the earlier 1-2-3 performs the operation. Operations with the same priority number are performed sequentially from left to right. A precedence order can be overridden by enclosing an operation in parentheses; 1-2-3 will perform the operations inside the parentheses first.

Operator	Function	Priority
( )	Parenthesized operation	1
^	Exponentiation	2
* or /	Multiplication or division	3
+ or -	Addition or subtraction	4
= or <>	Equal-to or not-equal-to	5
< or >	Less-than or greater-than	5
<=	Less-than-or-equal-to	5
>=	Greater-than-or-equal-to	5
#NOT#	Logical NOT	6
#AND#	Logical AND	7
#OR#	Logical OR	7
&	String concatenation	7

Using Functions

In our example, writing a formula that adds the contents of three columns is not too difficult or lengthy a task. But imagine having to add 20 columns! For this reason 1-2-3 has an inbuilt summation function (for others see Appendix B) in the form of @SUM( ) which can be used to add any number of cells.

To illustrate how this function can be used, move the cell pointer to E5 and type

@SUM(

which changes the mode indicator to VALUE, then use the arrow keys to move the cell pointer (note that pressing an arrow key changes the mode indicator to POINT) to the start of the summation range (B5 in this case), press

<.>   (period) to anchor the starting point of the range

and use the arrow keys to move the cell pointer to the end of the summation range (in this case D5). What appears under the cell indicator is the entry

@SUM(B5..D5

which has to be completed by typing the closing bracket ')' and pressing <Enter>.

Now use the 'Copy' command to replicate the function from cell E5 into the target range E8 through E13. To achieve this move the cell pointer to E5 and press

/	to reveal the menus
C	to select **Copy**
\<Enter>	to confirm highlighted copy range
\<Down>	to move to beginning of target range
\<.>	to anchor the first target cell
\<Down>	to select and highlight target range
\<Enter>	to confirm target range.

Immediately this command is confirmed, its execution causes the actual sums of the 'relative' columns to appear on the target area. Notice that when the cell pointer is on E5 the function target range is B5..D5, while when the cell pointer is moved to E8 the function target range changes to B8..D8 which indicates that copying formulae with this method causes the 'relative' target range to be copied. Had the 'absolute' target range been copied instead, the result of the various summations would have been wrong.

Next, complete the insertion of functions and formulae in the rest of the worksheet, noting that 'Total Cost' is the summation of rows 8 through 13, 'Profit' is the subtraction of 'Total Cost' from 'Consultancy', and that 'Cumulat' in row 19 refers to cumulative profit. Then, add another column to your worksheet to calculate (and place in column F) the average monthly values of earnings, costs, and profit, using the @AVG() function. The worksheet should look as shown below:

F5: @AVG(B5..D5)   READY

	A	B	C	D	E	F	G	H
1	PROJECT ANALYSIS: ADEPT CONSULTANTS LTD							
2								
3		Jan	Feb	Mar	1st Quart	Average		
4								
5	Consult:	14000	15000	16000	45000	15000		
6								
7	Costs:							
8	Wages	2000	3000	4000	9000	3000		
9	Travel	400	500	600	1500	500		
10	Rent	300	300	300	900	300		
11	Heat/Lght	150	200	150	500	166.6666		
12	Phone/Fax	250	300	350	900	300		
13	Adverts	1100	1200	1300	3600	1200		
14								
15	Tot Cost:	4200	5500	6700	16400	5466.666		
16								
17	Profit:	9800	9500	9300	28600	9533.333		
18								
19	Cumulat:	9800	19300	28600				
20								

Formatting Numbers:

Note the contents of F11, F15 and F17, under the 'Average' column, are no longer whole numbers. Furthermore, the number of digits after the decimal point is variable and depends on the available space - the width of the appropriate field.

To make our present worksheet more presentable, we need to format specific cells so that we are in control of what is printed out. To format the contents of a numeric cell or block of cells, highlight the starting target cell (in our example, F5) and press

/	to reveal the menus
R	to select **Range**
F	to select **Format**
F	to select **Fixed** number of decimal points - the default value is two decimal places
\<Enter\>	to select the default value
\<Down\>	to highlight target range (F5..F17 for this example)
\<Enter\>	to confirm target range.

It is possible that when numbers are formatted in this way, they might not fit into the default allocated space (width) of chosen cells. If that happens, you will know it as 1-2-3 fills such cells with asterisks (*).

Changing the Default Width of Cells:

To change the width of columns (in order to accommodate either large numbers or numbers expressed in the form of currency, press

/	to reveal the menus
W	to select **Worksheet**
C	to select **Column**
C	to select **Column-Range**
S	to select **Set-Width**

Release 2.3 asks you to highlight the column range first and then allows you to change the default value from 9 to, say, 12. With Release 2.2 the range selection comes after the width choice. If you are changing the width of a single column, highlight the column and repeat the above commands, but miss

out the **Column-Range** command. This command is new to Releases 2.2 & 2.3. Users of earlier releases will have to change the width of each column separately by recycling through the commands.

When the worksheet is 'Saved', the new column-width display format will be saved with it.

Changing Default Currency & Date Formats:
What follows is only relevant to earlier versions than Release 2.2 of Lotus 1-2-3. Releases 2.2 & 2.3 are already configured for the UK currency prefix and the European date format.

To change the default formats of currency and date of earlier releases from $ and MM-DD-YY to UK's £ and DD/MM/YY, press

/	to reveal the menus
W	to select **Worksheet**
G	to select **Global**
D	to select **Default**
O	to select **Other**
I	to select **International**
C	to select **Currency**. At this point the $ sign will be displayed. Backspace, and press
£	to select UK currency symbol
<Enter>	to confirm selection
P	to select **Prefix** so that the currency symbol prefixes numbers displayed in 'Currency' (£xxxxx.xx) format.
D	to select **Date**
B	to select option **B**.

To make these options permanent, return to a previous menu by pressing the <Esc> key once, and then press

U	to select and execute **Update**
Q	to **Quit**.

Dialogue Boxes:
If you are using Release 2.3, you can change settings using dialogue boxes rather than use the above menu commands. These replace the settings screens of Release 2.2. One such dialogue box, which was displayed on your screen while you

were selecting the **/Worksheet, Global, Default** commands, is
shown below:

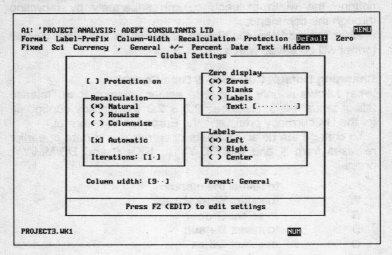

```
A1: 'PROJECT ANALYSIS: ADEPT CONSULTANTS LTD                    MENU
 Format  Label-Prefix  Column-Width  Recalculation  Protection  Default  Zero
 Fixed  Sci  Currency  ,  General  +/-  Percent  Date  Text  Hidden
 ──────────────────────────── Global Settings ───────────────
 ┌───────────────────────────────────────────────────────────┐
 │                              ┌─Zero display─────────────┐   │
 │         [ ] Protection on    │ (*) Zeros                │   │
 │                              │ ( ) Blanks               │   │
 │         ┌─Recalculation──────│ ( ) Labels               │   │
 │         │ (*) Natural        │     Text: [·········]    │   │
 │         │ ( ) Rowwise        └──────────────────────────┘   │
 │         │ ( ) Columnwise                                     │
 │         │                    ┌─Labels──────────────────┐   │
 │         │ [x] Automatic      │ (*) Left                 │   │
 │         │                    │ ( ) Right                │   │
 │         │ Iterations: [1·]   │ ( ) Center               │   │
 │         └────────────────    └──────────────────────────┘   │
 │                                                             │
 │         Column width: [9··]      Format: General            │
 ├─────────────────────────────────────────────────────────────┤
 │              Press F2 <EDIT> to edit settings               │
 └─────────────────────────────────────────────────────────────┘
 PROJECT3.WK1                                        NUM
```

A dialogue box shows the current settings for a particular task.
These settings can be changed with either the keyboard or the
mouse, or you can select commands from the menu above the
dialogue box.

Dialogue boxes offer you the following facilities for selecting
settings:

- Option buttons - you can select one option button from a
  group of option buttons by using the mouse to click it. A
  selected button is marked with an asterisk (*) next to the
  option.

- Check boxes - you can select one or more options (or
  none) from a group of option check boxes. A selected
  check box is marked with an x next to the option.

- Text boxes - you type entries in text boxes which can
  include numbers, range names, or text, depending on
  what the command requires.

30

Displaying Numbers in Currency Format:

To display numbers in a range of cells in currency format, no matter which release of Lotus 1-2-3 you are using, you must first format the range of cells to the 'Currency' format. For earlier versions than Release 2.2, you must also change the 'Default Currency' format, as discussed above.

Thus, to change the display of the numbers in row 5 of our worksheet, move the cell pointer to B5 and press

/	to reveal the menus
R	to select **Range**
F	to select **Format**
C	to select **Currency** number of decimal points - the default value is two decimal places
<Enter>	to select the default value
<Right>	to highlight range (B5..F5 for this example)
<Enter>	to confirm target range.

Printing a Worksheet

To print a worksheet, make sure that the printer is switched on and that the cell pointer is in the 'Home' position and the worksheet mode is on READY. Then, press

/	to reveal the menus
P	to select **Print**
P	to select **Printer**
R	to select **Range**
<Esc>	to deselect previous range selection (or automatic range selection in the case of Releases 2.2 & 2.3)
<.>	to anchor range from required position
<Arrows>	to move cell pointer to the bottom right-hand corner of the rectangle you wish to print
<Enter>	to confirm selection
G	to select **Go**

which should start printing. It is assumed here that you have configured your system to your printer. If you have not done this configuration (see next section) your printer might not respond to your print commands. On completion of the printout, press

Q	to select **Quit**

and return to the READY mode.

A request to print again, will automatically remember the previous range. If you require a different range, then when the highlighted rectangular area appears on screen, as a result of selecting the **Range** command, cancel the current range by pressing the <Esc> key, then move the cell pointer to the required starting position (top left-hand corner) of target area, and press

<.>   to anchor top left hand corner of rectangle
<Arrows>   to move the cell pointer to the bottom right-hand corner of rectangle you require to print
<Enter>   to confirm selection

Carry out the suggested formatting changes to column F of worksheet PROJECT2 and then arrange for the £ sign to prefix the consultancy entries in row 5. You will have to have changed the default 'Currency' format of your worksheet in order to do this successfully. Then, save the resultant worksheet as PROJECT3.

```
A1: 'PROJECT ANALYSIS: ADEPT CONSULTANTS LTD                    READY

        A       B        C        D        E         F          G
 1  PROJECT ANALYSIS: ADEPT CONSULTANTS LTD
 2
 3              Jan      Feb      Mar    1st Quart   Average
 4  ================================================================
 5  Consult:  £14,000  £15,000  £16,000  £45,000  £15,000.00
 6
 7  Costs:
 8  Wages       2000     3000     4000     9000    3000.00
 9  Travel       400      500      600     1500     500.00
10  Rent         300      300      300      900     300.00
11  Heat/Lght    150      200      150      500     166.67
12  Phone/Fax    250      300      350      900     300.00
13  Adverts     1100     1200     1300     3600    1200.00
14
15  Tot Cost:   4200     5500     6700    16400    5466.67
16  ================================================================
17  Profit:     9800     9500     9300    28600    9533.33
18  ================================================================
19  Cumulat:    9800    19300    28600
20  ================================================================
PROJECT3.WK1                 UNDO                           NUM
```

The Print Settings Menu:
If you are using Release 2.2 or 2.3, then the program automatically sets the printer range when you select the

/Print, Printer

command, to what it can print on the predefined size paper, which is what can be displayed on your screen. This information is displayed in the 'Print Settings' menu, as shown on the next page.

In the case of Release 2.2, the following screen is displayed:

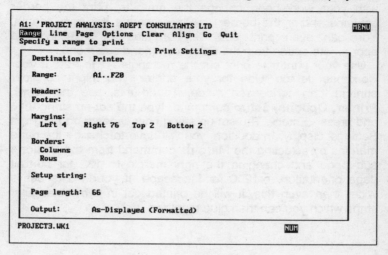

```
A1: 'PROJECT ANALYSIS: ADEPT CONSULTANTS LTD                    MENU
Range Line Page Options Clear Align Go Quit
Specify a range to print
                         ── Print Settings ──
     Destination:  Printer

     Range:        A1..FZ0

     Header:
     Footer:

     Margins:
       Left 4    Right 76   Top 2   Bottom 2

     Borders:
       Columns
       Rows

     Setup string:

     Page length:  66

     Output:       As-Displayed (Formatted)

PROJECT3.WK1                                         NUM
```

The corresponding screen for Release 2.3 is as follows:

```
A1: 'PROJECT ANALYSIS: ADEPT CONSULTANTS LTD                    MENU
Range Line Page Options Clear Align Go Quit
Specify a range to print
                         ── Print Settings ──
     Range: [A1..FZ0 ········]      ┌─Destination─────────────────┐
                                    │ (*) Printer    ( ) Encoded file│
     ┌─Margins────────────┐         │ ( ) Text file  ( ) Background │
     │ Left:  [4··] Top:    [2·]│    │                              │
     │ Right: [76·] Bottom: [2·]│    │ File name: [··················]│
     └────────────────────┘         └──────────────────────────────┘

     ┌─Borders────────────┐
     │ Columns: [··············]│    Page length: [66·]
     │ Rows:    [··············]│
     └────────────────────┘         Setup string: [·············]

     Header: [································]   [ ] Unformatted pages
     Footer: [································]   [ ] List entries

     Interface: Parallel 1          Name: IBM Graphics printer and Qu...

              Press F2 (EDIT) to edit settings

PROJECT3.WK1                                         NUM
```

33

You could 'Clear' all or just specific entries on this 'Print Settings' menu by selecting the **Clear** command from the displayed sub-menu. Other 'Print Settings' options can be changed or added to by the selection of the **Options** command which allows you to type the header and footer to be printed with your worksheet, change the margins, print the border columns and/or the border rows, or change the page length. You can even print out 'Cell-Formulas' by selecting the appropriate option from the **Other** command sub-menu.

Use your printer to print out the rectangle A1 to F20. If your worksheet is too wide for your printer, you might consider printing it in condensed mode. To do this, use the **\Print, Printer, Options, Setup** command, type the set-up string **\015** and press <Enter>. The set-up string now appears on the 'Print Settings' display. In addition, you will have to change the page margins by selecting the **Margins** command from the **Options** sub-menu and changing the right margin to 132 for portrait page orientation, or 200 for landscape. If your worksheet is wider than even this, it will be printed out in two rectangular strips which you can then glue together.

3. ADDING WORKSHEET SKILLS

We will now use the worksheet saved under PROJECT3 (see end of previous chapter) to show how we can add to it, rearrange information in it and freeze titles in order to make entries easier, before going on to discuss more advanced topics. If you haven't saved PROJECT3 on disc, it will be necessary for you to enter the information shown below into 1-2-3 so that you can benefit from what is to be introduced at this point. Having done this, do save it under PROJECT3 before going on with the suggested alterations.

If you have saved PROJECT3, then enter 1-2-3 and when the mode indicator reads READY, press

/	to reveal the menus
F	to select **File**
R	to select **Retrieve**

and highlight PROJECT3. On pressing <Enter>, the worksheet is displayed on the screen as shown below.

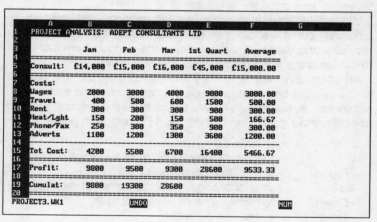

What we would like to do now is to add some more information to the worksheet with the insertion of another quarter's figures in columns between E and F.

35

Controlling Cell Contents

In general, you can insert or delete columns and rows in a worksheet, copy cell contents (including formulae) from one part of the worksheet to another, and freeze titles in order to make entries into cells easier.

The /Worksheet Insert Command:

To insert columns into a worksheet, move the cell pointer into the column where insertion is required (in this case F1) and press

/	to reveal the menus
W	to select **Worksheet**
I	to select **Insert**
C	to select **Column** which asks for range
<Right>	to highlight range F1..I1
<Enter>	to confirm range selection and execute.

On execution, empty cells are inserted into the worksheet in the requested range, and in this particular case, the column headed 'Average' now appears in column J.

We could now start entering information into the empty columns, but if we did this first, we would then have to first replicate and then edit appropriately the various formulae used to calculate the various results for the first quarter.

An alternative way is to copy everything from the first quarter to the second and then only edit the actual numeric information within the various columns. We will choose this second method to achieve our goal. First highlight cell B3 and then press

/	to reveal the menus
C	to select **Copy** which asks for range
<Right>	to highlight columns B3..E3
<.>	to anchor top right-hand corner of rectangle
<Down>	to highlight block of rows 3 to 20
<Enter>	to confirm selection
<Right>	to highlight cell F3
<Enter>	to confirm selection and execute.

Now edit the copied headings 'Jan', 'Feb', 'Mar', and '1st Quart' to 'Apr', 'May', 'Jun', and '2nd Quart'.

Note that by the time the highlighted bar is moved to column I, the 'titles' in column A have scrolled to the left and are outside the viewing screen area. This will make editing of numeric information very difficult if we can't see what refers to what. Therefore, before we attempt any further editing, it would be a good idea to use the 'Title' command ability of 1-2-3 to freeze the titles in column A of our present worksheet.

Freezing Titles on Screen:
To freeze column (or row) headings on a worksheet, move the cell pointer a cell to the right (or below) the column (or row) which you want to freeze the titles on the screen, and press

/	to reveal the menus
W	to select **Worksheet**
T	to select **Titles**
V (or H)	to select **Vertical** (or **Horizontal**)

which will automatically set the headings to the left (or above) the cell pointer's current position. Moving around the worksheet, leaves the headings frozen on the screen. Any attempt to enter the frozen area causes the speaker to bleep.

Now implement the above changes and change the numeric information on your worksheet into what is shown below.

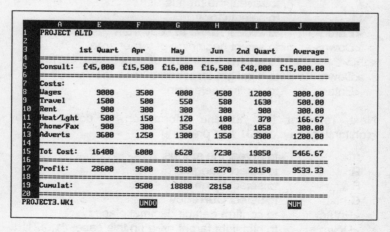

Note: If you examine this worksheet carefully, you will notice that two errors have occurred; one of these has to do with the average calculation in column J, while the other has to do with the accumulated values in the second quarter.

Non-Contiguous Address Range:
The calculations of average values in column J of the previous worksheet are wrong because the range values in the formula are still those entered for the first quarter only. To correct these, highlight cell J5 and edit the formula shown in the control panel from

@AVG(B5..D5)

to

@AVG(B5..D5,F5..H5)

which on pressing <Enter> changes the value shown in cell J5. Note the way the argument of the function is written when non-contiguous address ranges are involved. Here we have two contiguous address ranges B5..D5 and F5..H5 which we separate with a comma.

Now replicate the formula to the J8..J13 cell range by highlighting cell J5 and pressing

/	to reveal the menus
C	to select **Copy**
<Enter>	to accept range to copy from
<Down>	to select beginning of target area
<.>	to anchor beginning of target area
<Down>	to highlight target area
<Enter>	to confirm selection.

Next, reformat the numeric information in column J by highlighting, say, cell J1 and pressing

/	to reveal the menus
R	to select **Range**
F	to select **Format**
C	to select **Currency**
<Enter>	to confirm default decimal places
<Down>	to highlight target area (in this case, J1..J21)
<Enter>	to confirm selection.

Relative and Absolute Cell Addresses:

Entering a mathematical expression into the worksheet, such as the formula in cell C19 which was

    +B19+C17

causes 1-2-3 to interpret it as 'add the contents of cell one column to the left of the current position, to the contents of cell two rows above the current position'. In this way, when the formula was later replicated into cell address D19, the contents of the cell relative to the left position of D19 (i.e. C19) and the contents of the cell two rows above it (i.e. D17) is used, instead of the original cell addresses entered in C19. This is relative addressing.

To see the effect of relative versus absolute addressing, type in cell E19 the formula

    +E5-E15

which will be interpreted as relative addressing. Now, add another row to your worksheet, namely 'Profit/Q:' in row 21 to calculate the profit per quarter. Before you are able to enter the new label, however, you must first unfreeze the titles by pressing

/	to reveal the menus
W	to select **Worksheet**
T	to select **Titles**
C	to select **Clear**.

Having entered the label in cell A21, copy the formula in cell E19 to cell E21, using the /**Copy** command. The displayed calculated value in E21 is, of course, wrong because the cell references in the copied formula are now given as

    +E7-E17

as the references were copied relatively. Next, change the formula in E19 by editing it to

    +$E$5-$E$15

which is interpreted as absolute addressing. Copying this into cell E21 calculates the correct result; the cell references in the formula in E21 have not changed from those of cell E19.

The $ sign must prefix both the column reference and the row reference. Mixed cell addressing is permitted; as for example when a column address reference is needed as absolute, while a row address reference is needed as relative. In such a case, only the column letter is prefixed by the $ sign.

Finally, correct the formula in cells F19 and I19 in order to obtain the correct results shown below.

```
I21: +$I$5-$I$15+E21                                              READY

        A       E        F        G        H        I         J
2
3             1st Quart   Apr      May      Jun   2nd Quart  Average
4   ================================================================
5  Consult:  £45,000  £15,500  £16,000  £16,500  £48,000  £15,500.00
6   ================================================================
7  Costs:
8  Wages       9000     3500     4000     4500    12000   £3,500.00
9  Travel      1500      500      550      580     1630     £521.67
10 Rent         900      300      300      300      900     £300.00
11 Heat/Lght    500      150      120      100      370     £145.00
12 Phone/Fax    900      300      350      400     1050     £325.00
13 Adverts     3600     1250     1300     1350     3900   £1,250.00
14  ----------------------------------------------------------------
15 Tot Cost:  16400     6000     6620     7230    19850   £6,041.67
16  ================================================================
17 Profit:    28600     9500     9380     9270    28150   £9,458.33
18  ----------------------------------------------------------------
19 Cumulat:   28600    38100    47480    56750    56750
20  ================================================================
21 Profit/Q:  28600                              56750
PROJECT4.WK1              UNDO                            NUM
```

The /Move Command:

In order to improve the printed output of the example we have been discussing, we could move the caption to somewhere in the middle of the worksheet so that is centrally placed when we print it out. To do this, move the cell pointer to A1 and move the caption by pressing

/	to reveal the menus
M	to select **Move**
<Enter>	to select default range to move
<Right>	to select target range (say D1..D1)
<Enter>	to confirm target range and execute.

Now freeze again the titles in column A, press the <Home> key and save the resultant worksheet as PROJECT4.

Working with Files

So far, we have discussed the /**File, Save** and /**File, Retrieve** commands which were used to respectively save to disc and load into memory worksheet files. Filenames were restricted to eight alphanumeric characters, with worksheet files having the three letter extension .WK1 automatically added to them. However, 1-2-3 can deal with lots of differently formatted files which are recognised by their different extensions.

Types of Files:

In addition to the worksheet files .WK1, 1-2-3 can create worksheet back-up , graph, and text files. Such files are created when you carry out certain processes. These are:

Extension	Process
.WK1	Worksheet files produced when you use the /**File, Save** or /**File, Xtract** command
.BAK	Worksheet back-up files which store previous versions of worksheets. These are created when you use the /**File, Save** or /**File, Xtract** command, specify an existing worksheet filename, and then select the **Backup** option from the menu
.PIC	Graph files produced when you use the /**Graph, Save** command to store graphs in picture format
.PRN	Text or print files produced when you use the /**Print, File** command which stores worksheet data in text or ASCII format on disc.

If you want to find out what type of 1-2-3 files are held on the currently logged drive\directory, use the /**File, List** command. You can then select one of the following options:

Worksheet	Lists worksheet files (*.WKS, *.WK1, and *.WK3, corresponding to release 1A; release 2.0, 2.01, 2.2 & 2.3; and release 3.0 & 3.1, respectively) in the current directory
Print	Lists print files (*.PRN) in the current directory
Graph	Lists graph files (*.PIC) in the current directory
Other	Lists all Files (*.*) in the current directory

Linked	Lists all files on disc that are linked to the current worksheet.

Linking Files

A new feature of 1-2-3 Releases 2.2 & 2.3 is file linking. This allows you to use values from cells in other worksheets (which have been saved on disc) into the current worksheet (the worksheet in memory). As the current file receives data, it is referred to as the target file, while the file that the formula refers to is called the source file.

File linking can save you the trouble of having to constantly update worksheets, such as a consolidation report which you might have built on a separate worksheet for the sake of security. Once files have been linked, 1-2-3 copies the value of the cell in the source file into the cell of the target file which is then automatically updated whenever the target file is retrieved or you issue the **Link-Refresh** command while working on the target file (more about this later).

As an example of linking files together we will work through an exercise to carry out a consolidation operation. The file we would like to construct is shown below. But before you start typing information in order to create this new file, it might be worth considering whether you will save yourself some time by perhaps copying part of an existing file. How to do this is explained overleaf.

```
C6: (C0) [W12] +<<PROJECT4.WK1>>I5                          READY
```

	A	B	C	D	E	F
1	ADEPT CONSULTANTS LTD					
2	PROJECT ANALYSIS - 1990 SUMMARY					
3						
4		1st Quart	2nd Quart	3rd Quart	4th Quart	TOTAL
5						
6	Consult:	£45,000	£48,000			£93,000
7						
8	Costs:					
9	Wages	£9,000	£12,000			£21,000
10	Travel	£1,500	£1,630			£3,130
11	Rent	£900	£900			£1,800
12	Heat/Lght	£500	£370			£870
13	Phone/Fax	£900	£1,050			£1,950
14	Adverts	£3,600	£3,900			£7,500
15						
16	Tot Costs	£16,400	£19,850			£36,250
17						
18	Profit	£28,600	£28,150			£56,750
19						
20						

```
PROJECTS.WK1                  UNDO                    NUM
```

42

Copying a File into Memory:

Before you can copy a file into memory, use the **/Worksheet, Erase, Yes** command (discussed previously) to clear the computer's memory. Having done so, press

/	to reveal the menus
F	to select **File**
C	to select **Combine**
C	to select **Copy**
N	to select **Named/Specified-Range**

then specify range A1..A18, and type the filename PROJECT4. You could now type the missing label in cell A1 and the five column headings in row 4, then move the cell pointer into A2 and use the **/Worksheet, Insert** command to insert another row, so there is room for the additional label 'PROJECT ANALYSIS - 1990 SUMMARY'.

Format of Linking Formulae:

Cell references between different files are shown with the path and filename, included in double angular brackets (<<...>>), placed before the cell address.

The screen dump of the consolidation sheet displayed on the previous page shows how the linkage between files is effected. When the cell pointer is in C6 (the 2nd quarter's consultancy income), the formula is

+<<PROJECT4.WK1>>I5

indicating that this cell (C6 in the target file) has been linked to cell I5 of the source file PROJECT4 which is to be found on the disc in the currently logged drive and directory.

If the source file you are linking to is on another drive, then the full drive\path must also be given between the first double angular brackets and the filename. For example, to link a cell in the current (target) worksheet to, say, cell A1 in the source file, called 'myfile', to be found in the C: drive in subdirectory \lot123v2\data, you will have to type

+<<C:\lot123v3\data\myfile>>A1

in the highlighted cell of the current worksheet. Note that if you don't include the filename extension .WK1, 1-2-3 will add it for you.

Linked formulae can be edited, or copied from one part of the consolidation worksheet to another, just like ordinary formulae. Thus, after completing the entry, editing, and copying of linked formulae, save the consolidation worksheet under the filename PROJECT5.

Refreshing Linkages:

Whenever a target file that is linked to another file is retrieved into memory with the **/File, Retrieve** command, the formulae that contain the linkages are automatically 'updated'. However, if you are sharing files in a multiuser environment, other users might change the source files while you are viewing a target file. To make quite sure that the target file contains all the latest changes, select the **/File, Admin, Link-Refresh** command. This command recalculates formulae in active files that include references to other files on disk.

Note: When attempting to link files, try to observe the following restrictions and suggestions:

- Do not include a linking formula in another formula
- Always include a path as part of the file reference, because should you change the current directory, 1-2-3 will not be able to find the source file and will display ERR in the target cell
- Remember not to erase or rename the source file, or a referenced range name, otherwise 1-2-3 will display ERR in the target cell
- Always use a range name (see next chapter) as the cell reference in a linking formula rather than making direct reference to a cell address, because if you move the source cell to a different location within the source worksheet, 1-2-3 will not be able to locate the new cell address and will display ERR in the target cell.

Finally, if you have more than two files linked, remember that the order in which you retrieve these files is important in correctly refreshing their links. For example, if worksheet A depends on worksheet B, which in turn depends on worksheet C, changing data in worksheet C will not be reflected in worksheet A, unless you first retrieve and save worksheet B.

4. SPREADSHEET GRAPHS

Lotus 1-2-3 allows you to represent information in graphical form which makes data more accessible to non-Lotus users who might not be familiar with the spreadsheet format. In any case, the well known saying 'a picture is worth a thousand words', applies equally well to graphs and figures.

Types of Charts

Lotus 1-2-3 Release 2.2 allows five different types of charts to be drawn, each illustrating up to six separate ranges of data. Release 2.3 adds two more main types, and also allows for special effects, like plotting bars sideways or adding a 3D-effect, which increases quite considerably the overall number of charts available to the user. You can display dots, lines or bars, and you can add titles, legends, labels, and a grid. These charts (you can have several per worksheet) can be displayed on the screen or can be saved separately on disc so that they can be sent to the printer later. The types of charts, or graphs, available are:

Release 2.2
Line   Bar   XY   Stack-Bar   Pie

Release 2.3
As above, plus   HLCO   Mixed   Features

On selecting one of these, 1-2-3 expects you to define the X data range, followed by up to six (A - F) y-axis data ranges. The five graph-types are normally used when we would like to describe the following relationships between data:

Line   for showing changes is data over time - up to six sets, A - F, can be drawn against an x-axis range of labels.

Bar   for comparing differences in data - up to six sets, A - F, can be drawn against an x-axis range of labels.

XY   for showing scatter relationships between X and Y - up to six points on the chart (using the A - F data range) can be plotted against an x-axis range of values.

Stack-Bar	for comparing cumulative data - up to six sets, A - F, can be drawn against an x-axis range labels. The data in the A range appear at the bottom of the stack with data in the F range appearing at the very top.
Pie	for comparing parts with the whole. Use the X range for pie-slice labels, the A range for the pie-slice values, and the B range for allocating colour or hatch patterns to the slices.
HLCO	for showing the extreme high and low fluctuations of data values with time, together with their corresponding closing and opening values during that period. The X data range is used to specify the x-axis labels, with ranges A, B, C and D being used for the sets of high, low, close, and open values, respectively. The E range can be used as a set of bars below the HLCO area, while the F range can be used as a line in the HLCO area. This type of chart is useful for describing opening and closing trading figures of shares in the stock market.
Mixed	for showing different types of data on the same graph; they are combinations of bar and line graphs. The X data range is used for the x-axis labels, while ranges A, B, and C are used as sets of bars, and ranges D, E, and F are used as sets of lines.

The Features option of the /**Graph, Type** command, offers the following five charting capabilities:

| Vertical | Displays a horizontal x-axis across the bottom of the graph, with a vertical y-axis along the left edge of the graph. This is the default choice. |
| Horizontal | Displays the chart rotated by 90 degrees, with the x-axis vertical and the y-axis horizontal. |

Stacked	Displays corresponding data-range values in stacked form. This feature can be used with line, bar, XY and mixed charts.
Frame	Controls how much of the graph 1-2-3 surrounds by a frame, adds or removes gutters, or adds or removes zero lines.
3D-Effect	Adds a three-dimensional effect on your bar, stacked bar, and mixed graphs.

Graphs can not be displayed at the same time as the worksheet (unless you use the Allways add-in or Wysiwyg module) because graphs use the graphics mode of your computer while worksheets use the text mode. Nevertheless, once the preliminary definition of data and selection of the type of graph you would like to see is made, viewing graphs is quite easy; simply press the **F10** key. As graphs are dynamic, any changes made to the data on the worksheet are automatically reflected on the already defined graphs.

Preparing for a Line Graph:
In order to illustrate some of the graphing capabilities of 1-2-3, we will now plot the 'Profit' from consultancies graph of the PROJECT4 worksheet. First we need to define the type of graph to be displayed followed by the range of the data we want to graph. However, the specified range of data to be graphed must be contiguous for each graph. But in our example, the range of data is split into two areas; Jan-Mar (occupying cell positions B3..D3), and Apr-Jun (occupying cell positions F3..H3), with the corresponding profit values in cells B17..D17 and F17..H17. Thus, to create an appropriate contiguous data range, we must first replicate the labels and values of these two range areas in another area of the worksheet (say, beginning in cell B21 for the actual month labels and B22 for the values of the corresponding profit).

To do this, use /**Worksheet, Titles, Clear** command to unfreeze the titles in column A, then select /**Range, Erase** to erase the contents of row 21 so that all cells of interest are visible on the screen at once. Labels can be copied in the usual way with the /**Copy** command. However, before you start copying the profit row, stop and consider what will happen if you

do so. As these cells contain formulae, using the /**Copy**
command would cause the relative cell addresses to adjust to
the new locations and each formula will then recalculate a new
value for each cell, which will give wrong results.

The /Range Value Command:

This command copies only the value in a cell and not its
underlying formula which calculated this value. To do this, make
sure that PROJECT4 is your current worksheet and that the
mode indicator is on READY, then highlight cell B17 and press

/	to reveal the menus
R	to select **Range**
V	to select **Value**
<Right>	to highlight the columns corresponding to the Jan-Mar range
<Enter>	to confirm range selection, at which point you'll be asked to enter range to copy to
<Down>	to move and highlight the beginning of the range to copy data values to (B22 in this case)
<Enter>	to confirm and execute the copy of data.

Now repeat the same procedure for the profit data in the
Apr-Jun range, but copy them into E22 to form a contiguous
data range. Finally, add labels for 'Months' and 'Profit' in cells
A21 and A22, as shown below, and save the resultant
worksheet under the filename PROJECT6.

	A	B	C	D	E	F	G	H
3		Jan	Feb	Mar	1st Quart	Apr	May	Jun
5	Consult:	£14,000	£15,000	£16,000	£45,000	£15,500	£16,000	£16,500
7	Costs:							
8	Wages	2000	3000	4000	9000	3500	4000	4500
9	Travel	400	500	600	1500	500	550	580
10	Rent	300	300	300	900	300	300	300
11	Heat/Lght	150	200	150	500	150	120	100
12	Phone/Fax	250	300	350	900	300	350	400
13	Adverts	1100	1200	1300	3600	1250	1300	1350
15	Tot Cost:	4200	5500	6700	16400	6000	6620	7230
17	Profit:	9800	9500	9300	28600	9500	9380	9270
19	Cumulat:	9800	19300	28600	28600	38100	47480	56750
21	Months:	Jan	Feb	Mar	Apr	May	Jun	
22	Profit:	9800	9500	9300	9500	9380	9270	

PROJECT6.WK1   UNDO   NUM

48

The /Graph Command:

We can now proceed with the definition of the type of graph to be drawn. To do this, make sure that the mode indicator is on READY and press

/	to reveal the menus
G	to select **Graph** and display the 'Type' sub-menu. If you are using Release 2.2 or 2.3, the Graph Settings screen will also be displayed
T	to select **Type**
L	to select **Line** graph.

The Graph menu then reappears so that you can first select the X (horizontal) range, and then up to 6 vertical ranges (A through F) in a single graph. In this case, we only need to select one vertical range as we are dealing with the profit from consultancies only. Thus, first define the X range by pressing

X	to select the X-range
\<Arrows\>	to highlight the beginning of the range
\<.\>	to anchor the beginning of the X range
\<Arrows\>	to highlight entire range (B21..G21)
\<Enter\>	to confirm range selection
A	to select the first Y range
\<Arrows\>	to highlight beginning of the A range
\<.\>	to anchor the beginning of the A range
\<Arrows\>	to highlight entire range (B22..G22)
\<Enter\>	to confirm range selection

If you are using 1-2-3 Release 2.2 or 2.3, as you are issuing the above commands, the information typed will be transferred automatically to the Graph Setting or dialogue screen (depending on which release you are using), which by now should look as shown on the next page.

To view the line graph, select the **View** command from the /**Graph** sub-menu, or if 1-2-3 is in READY mode, press the **F10** function key. At this point, your screen should clear and a line graph, as shown on the next page, should appear on it. Should your computer bleep instead, then you must have made a mistake when defining either the type of graph or the data ranges. If that happens, then press the \<Esc\> key to return to the **Graph** menu, select **Reset** and start again. If you don't use

Reset you will find that 1-2-3 remembers the previously defined range settings, which might be rather useful to you if you are defining another graph type which uses the same range settings.

The Graph Settings screen of Release 2.2, is shown below:

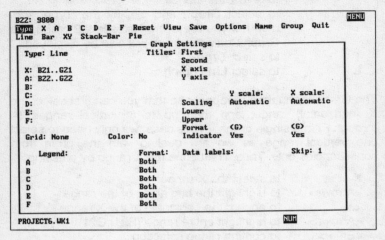

The corresponding dialogue box of Release 2.3 is shown below:

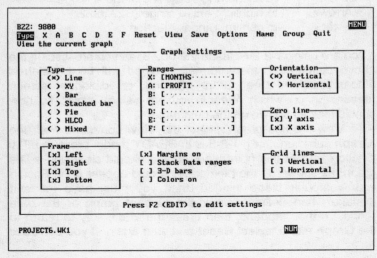

The resultant line graph, whether you use Release 2.2 or 2.3, is the same, as shown below:

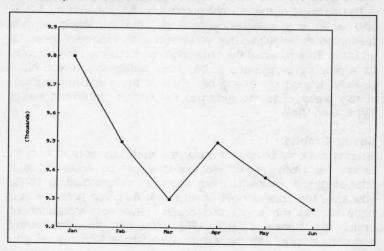

Naming Ranges and Graphs

It is often more convenient to 'name' a range of data and then use the name rather than the cell addresses in subsequent worksheet operations, including graphing. To illustrate this point, select the **/Graph, Reset, Graph** command to clear all current graph setting, then press <Esc> to return to the main 1-2-3 menu.

Next, choose the **Range, Name, Create** command and type the name MONTHS. You are now asked to enter the range for this name, which in our case is B21..G21. Then repeat the previous command to name range B22..G22 as PROFIT. Next, select the **/Graph, Type, Line** command and type in for the **X** data-range the actual name MONTHS (don't point to the label with the same name in the worksheet, as its selection will not work), and for the **A** data-range the name PROFIT. Selecting the **View** command now displays the familiar line graph.

Once the correct graph has been successfully displayed on screen, you can 'Name' it for future use. To name a graph, select the **Name** command from the **Graph** sub-menu which displays a list of options which lets you **Create, Use** or **Delete** a named graph, **Reset** (delete), or create a **Table** of named graphs. Select **Create** which will prompt you for a graph name. In this case, type the name PROFIT_LINE and press <Enter>.

The settings of the current graph are remembered by 1-2-3, and when you select new settings, the current ones are presented as default so that you can reuse as many of these as you like. This reduces the time required to define new settings for a graph that happens to be rather similar to one you have already defined. To see a bar chart of the same information, simply press <Esc> to return to the **Graph** menu and select **Type, Bar, View**.

Saving Graphs:

Graphs will only be saved under the particular spreadsheet in which they were created (so that they can be accessed at a later stage), if you name them and then, before quitting 1-2-3, you save the spreadsheet again under its given name. If you have named the suggested graph, save your spreadsheet under the filename PROJECT6. You can save as many separate graphs with the same spreadsheet filename as you like, provided you gave each one a different 'name', using the **/Graph, Name** command. To select any graph and make it current, choose the **/Graph, Use** command (press **F3** to see a list of saved chart names in tabular form, if you have defined lots of them), highlight the required one and press <Enter>.

Note: The **/Graph, Name** command is different from the **/Graph, Save** command. **/Graph, Save** creates a separate file of the current graph on the data disc so that it can be printed with the Lotus 1-2-3 **PrintGraph** program which is one of the options available in the 'Lotus Access System'.

Legends and Titles:

There are several options within the **/Graph, Options** sub-menu which allow you to add information on your graph.

The **/Graph, Options, Legend** selection, allows you to specify the wording of a legend which appears on the x-axis of your graph. In the case of our example, this was not required as the x-axis range itself was descriptive. Legends are not relevant to pie charts.

The **/Graph, Options, Titles** selection allows you to add a two-line title to the whole graph, or add annotation to the x and y axes. To add a title to the previous example, use the **/Graph,**

Options, Titles, First option. To annotate the Y axis, choose **/Graph, Options, Titles, Y**, type 'Profit' and press <Enter>.

Drawing a Multiple Bar Chart:

As an exercise, define graph settings for a new bar-type graph which deals with the monthly 'Costs' of Adept Consultants. Start by using the **/Range, Value** command to copy the various costs into a contiguous worksheet range at the bottom of the worksheet, say, starting at cell A23.

As there are six different costs, you must define data-ranges A to F inclusive, so that 6 different bars (corresponding to the six different costs) can be plotted for each month. Use the **/Range, Name, Create** command to name each cost range. Annotate and title your graph, and enter legends to mark the different cross-hatching patterns which represent the various costs. If you are using Release 2.01, the legends describing these costs must be as short as possible (with six costs use only a single letter), if the printout is to be correct.

With 1-2-3 Release 2.2 or 2.3, use the **/Range, Name, Create** command to name range B24..G30 as COSTS, as shown overleaf. Then, use the **/Graph, Group** command and type the range name COSTS, which causes 1-2-3 to ask whether to use the columns or the rows as data ranges. Select the **Rowwise** option. Next, use the **Options, Legend, Range** command and highlight the labels in range A25..A30. Only with 1-2-3 Release 2.2 or 2.3 can you select a range of legends. With previous versions you must specify each one separately.

```
G30: 1350
Enter name: COSTS                    Enter range: B24..G30           POINT
```

	A	B	C	D	E	F	G	H
15	Tot Cost:	4200	5500	6700	16400	6000	6620	7230
16								
17	Profit:	9800	9500	9300	28600	9500	9380	9270
18								
19	Cumulat:	9800	19300	28600	28600	38100	47480	56750
20								
21	Months:	Jan	Feb	Mar	Apr	May	Jun	
22	Profit:	9800	9500	9300	9500	9380	9270	
23	Costs:							
24	Months:	Jan	Feb	Mar	Apr	May	Jun	
25	Wages	2000	3000	4000	3500	4000	4500	
26	Travel	400	500	600	500	550	580	
27	Rent	300	300	300	300	300	300	
28	Heat/Lght	150	200	150	150	120	100	
29	Phone/Fax	250	300	350	300	350	400	
30	Adverts	1100	1200	1300	1250	1300	1350	
31								

Finally, use the **Title** option to give your bar chart a title and to annotate the two axes, as shown in the following Graph Settings screen:

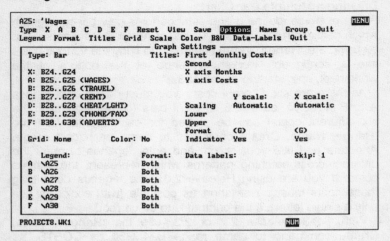

Don't forget to use the /**Graph, Name, Create** command to give this graph a name - call it COSTS_BAR. The completed graph should look as follows:

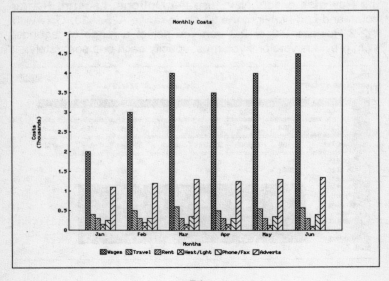

After viewing the bar chart, use the **/Graph, Save** command to save it as a .PIC file on disc, for possible use later with the **PrintGraph** program. Give this graph the name COSTS. The extension .PIC will be added automatically for you. Finally, save the worksheet graphs by saving the spreadsheet under the filename PROJECT7.

Using the **/Graph, Stack-Bar, 3D-Effect** command of Release 2.3, on the same graph settings as the previous multiple bar chart, you can obtain the following screen:

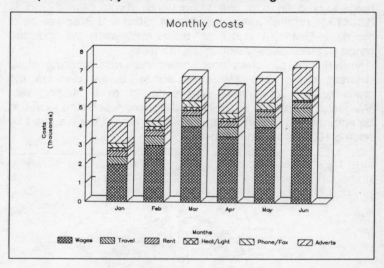

Drawing a Pie Chart:

As a second example, use the 'Average' values of the costs from your worksheet to plot a pie chart. It is advisable to use the **/Graph, Reset, Graph** command to clear all current graph setting, as the new chart you are about to put together is so different from the current one.

Again, define the new graph type as 'Pie' and then set the **X** range to the labels describing the costs (cells A8..A13), then set the **A** (first) range of data to the actual cost values (which are in cells J8..J13) and view the result. You will find that the different parts of the pie chart are all labelled with the words describing the various costs in the worksheet and that percentage values of each cost appear next to them.

Cross-hatching Code Numbers:

We need to provide code numbers for cross-hatching of the pie chart as Lotus 1-2-3 does not automatically shade the slices of a pie chart. The allowable codes are in fact from 0 to 7, each resulting with a different cross-hatching pattern. The codes must be inserted somewhere in the worksheet and the **B** (second) data-range should be set to them.

One way of creating automatically the required codes is to exploit the **/Data, Fill** command. The command first asks for a range to be defined for data filling, which in your case should be K8..K13., and then asks for the **Start**, **Step** and **Stop** values of the data. Use 1, 1 and 6 for these and watch the specified range fill automatically with these numbers.

Viewing the pie chart now shows the cross-hatching of its different slices. The pie chart shown below displays the cross-hatching obtainable with codes 1 to 6 starting with 'Wages' and going in a clockwise direction. A selected slice can be emphasized by detaching it from the rest of the pie chart by adding 100 to its code number.

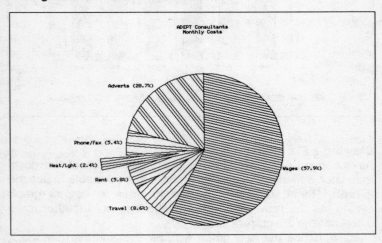

When you are satisfied with your efforts, don't forget to use the **Name, Create** command to give this chart the name COSTS_PIE, then save the worksheet under the filename PROJECT8, so that the graphs are saved with it.

56

The available cross-hatching patterns against their codes are shown below.

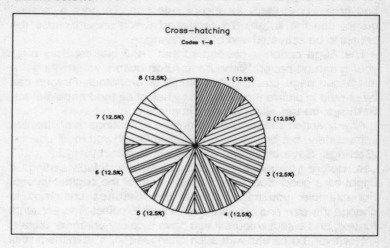

Using the PrintGraph Module

If you are the first person to use the Lotus PrintGraph module you must implement it to accept the 'Saved' graphs which now have the extension .PIC. To do this, quit the worksheet and select **PrintGraph** from the 'Lotus Access System' and select **Settings, Hardware** and **Graphs-Directory** and type

c:\lot123v2\data

followed by <Enter>. This assumes that you have saved the .PIC files in the **data** subdirectory of **\lot123v2** directory on the **c:** drive. Then select **Fonts-Directory** and type

c:\lot123v2

because the 'font' files are kept in the main Lotus 1-2-3 directory. Now select **Settings, Hardware** and then **Printer** to select the combination of printer and density of print required, then **Quit** to return to the Settings menu from where you should select **Save** followed by **Quit**.

From this point on, graphs can be printed on paper by selecting **Image-Select** and specifying the particular .PIC file you want to print by highlighting its name from those listed, pressing the <Spacebar> to mark it with the hash (#) character (at which point you could preview it on screen by pressing **F10**), and pressing <Enter> to accept selection. To print a marked graph, use the **Align, Go** command which should cause the printer to be activated and begin printing.

The **Align** option is needed so that 1-2-3 can correctly align your graph on paper. Without the **Align** option, you might get a misplaced page break in the middle of a printout. Graphs can be printed in different orientation by selecting the **Image-Select, Settings, Image, Size, Manual** command.

Any changes made to the PrintGraph settings are effective immediately, but before you leave PrintGraph you must use the **/Settings, Save** command if you want to retain them for future use. Before you make any changes to the default settings it might be a good idea if you made a note of the original values. For example, you might choose the **/Settings** command to change the size and proportion of a graph, select different fonts for text, and select colours if you have a colour printer or plotter.

However, be careful with such changes (don't save them until you are absolutely satisfied) as printing pie charts some time later might produce an egg shaped graph after 10 minutes of laborious printing if you change the proportion of the graph incorrectly. If you do make any such changes which you save and later discover they are not what you want, choose 'half size' graphs from the **/Settings, Size** menu, and save your choice. If you are not careful, you could end up wasting an awful lot of hours experimenting with PrintGraph. The reason is the slowness with which your printer draws such graphs.

The separateness of the PrintGraph program from the Lotus 1-2-3 program, causes a lot of other problems to users of Release 2.01 and earlier. For example, it is impossible to print a graph and the table of figures from which it was derived on the same sheet of paper. The Allways add-in which comes with Release 2.2 (or can be bought separately for earlier releases) and Wysiwyg that comes with Release 2.3, go a long way in rectifying this separation between two such vital programs. The use of the Allways add-in and Wysiwyg, which allow you to print tables of figures as well as graphs on the same page in any shape or form, is the subject of the next chapter. First, we discuss the Allways add-in (mainly for users of Release 2.2), followed by the Wysiwyg module for users of Release 2.3.

5. SPREADSHEET PUBLISHING

The Allways spreadsheet publishing add-in that comes with Lotus 1-2-3 Release 2.2, or which you can purchase separately for earlier releases of Lotus 1-2-3, and the Wysiwyg (what you see is what you get) module that comes with Lotus 1-2-3 Release 2.3, allow you to enhance the appearance of your worksheet both on screen and on paper; you can customise worksheet fonts, add text enhancements (such as bold and underline), shade worksheet ranges, change screen colours, etc. The printed output that you can achieve with either Allways or Wysiwyg is of high quality, whether you print reports, documents or graphs. Users of earlier versions of 1-2-3 can only benefit from this chapter if they have the Allways add-in which is suitable for their particular version of 1-2-3.

Before we discuss specific aspects of the Allways add-in or the Wysiwyg module, we need to prepare a worksheet and discuss some terminology common to both. This is done in the next two sections which you should read first, before you turn to the publishing module appropriate to your 1-2-3 release.

Preparing a Worksheet

To illustrate some of the spreadsheet publishing and graphing capabilities of Allways and Wysiwyg, we will now work on the consolidation worksheet (PROJECT5) of the small consulting company we discussed at the end of Chapter 3. However, before we can go on, you will need to complete the entries for the other two quarters of trading of the Adept Consultants' example into the PROJECT4 file and link the quarterly totals to the consolidation file of PROJECT5, which should then be saved as PROJECT9.

Of course, if you don't feel like doing this right now, you can always add manually the quarterly totals in the consolidation worksheet. However, for those who would like to do things properly and/or would like the opportunity to practice what they have learned so far, we list below the data needed in the PROJECT4 file to create the consolidation file. Having made the additions, use the /**Range, Name, Create** command to give the ranges used in the consolidation file relevant names. This is good practice, as discussed in the previous chapter.

Finally, having carried out the suggested changes, don't forget to save worksheet PROJECT4 under its original name.

	Jul	Aug	Sep	Oct	Nov	Dec
Consult:	17,000	16,000	16,500	18,000	20,000	22,000
Costs:						
Wages	4,000	4,000	4,500	4,000	4,500	5,500
Travel	450	400	550	550	600	650
Rent	300	300	300	300	300	300
Heat/Lght	80	60	90	130	170	240
Phone/Fax	330	170	250	380	400	450
Adverts	1,200	1.000	1,200	1,350	1,400	1,500

Next, retrieve the consolidation worksheet PROJECT5 and edit existing linking formulae by replacing references to actual cell ranges in the source file by named ranges, then add the additional linking formulae needed to fill the worksheet. Completing this work is quicker than imagined, provided you adopt a liberal use of the EDIT **(F2)** key and /**Copy** command. The final contents of the PROJECT9 file, should look as follows:

```
A1: [W12] 'ADEPT CONSULTANTS LTD                                    READY

        A         B           C           D           E           F
1   ADEPT CONSULTANTS LTD
2   PROJECT ANALYSIS - 1990 SUMMARY
3
4             1st Quart   2nd Quart   3rd Quart   4th Quart      TOTAL
5   =================================================================
6   Consult:    £45,000     £48,000     £49,500     £60,000    £282,500
7
8   Costs:
9   Wages        £9,000     £12,000     £12,500     £14,000     £47,500
10  Travel       £1,500      £1,630      £1,400      £1,800      £6,330
11  Rent           £900        £900        £900        £900      £3,600
12  Heat/Lght      £500        £370        £230        £540      £1,640
13  Phone/Fax      £900      £1,050        £750      £1,230      £3,930
14  Adverts      £3,600      £3,900      £3,400      £4,250     £15,150
15  ---------------------------------------------------------------
16  Tot Costs   £16,400     £19,850     £19,180     £22,720     £78,150
17  ---------------------------------------------------------------
18  Profit      £28,600     £28,150     £30,320     £37,280    £124,350
19  =================================================================
20
PROJECT9.WK1            UNDO                            NUM
```

Next, define a pie chart of the yearly costs and then save it as a .PIC file giving it the name YEARCOST. Later on, we will use this file when we discuss the individual publishing modules.

Font Styles

When you first use the Allways add-in or the Wysiwyg module, you will find that there are eight character fonts resident which you can use to enhance the looks of your worksheet. These fonts, called the font set, can be replaced with other typefaces of varied size from a list supplied with the appropriate module, or a library of soft fonts, if you happen to have purchased them from a third party.

There are two ways of specifying the size of a character font; a 'point' is approximately 1/72 of an inch, and determines the height of a character, while a 'pitch' is the number of characters that can fit horizontally in one inch. The spacing of a font is either 'fixed' (monospaced) or 'proportional'. With fixed spacing, each character takes up exactly the same space, while proportionally spaced characters take up different spacing (an 'i' or a 't' take up less space than a 'u' or a 'w'). Thus, the length of proportionally spaced text can vary depending on which letters it contains. However, numerals take up the same amount of space whether they have been specified as fixed or proportional.

Which fonts you choose is largely dependent on your printer. Here you can experiment to your heart's delight, but it will take time. One thing you must bear in mind is that 1-2-3 uses screen fonts to display characters on screen and printer fonts to print characters with a printer. If you choose printer fonts for which there are no screen fonts, 1-2-3 will use the nearest screen font to display your work on screen, which might not be exactly what you will see when you print your work.

The Allways Add-in - Release 2.2

Before you can load Allways into memory, you must have installed the add-in package according to the instructions accompanying the software (for the Allways add-in that comes with Release 2.2 of 1-2-3, see Chapter 1). Having done so, first load 1-2-3 and, when the program displays a blank worksheet and is in the READY mode, then

1. Use the /**Add-In** command
2. Select **Attach**
3. Choose the ALLWAYS.ADN (the first highlighted) file
4. Choose the **10** key, which is the APP4 (Alt+**F10**) key.

From this point on, you can either select the **Invoke** option to activate the attached add-in program immediately, or you can choose **Quit** to carry on with the normal functions of 1-2-3. The Allways add-in can be invoked at will, whenever 1-2-3 is in READY mode, by simply pressing Alt+**F10**. Although this key combination was initially set to display the /**Add-In** menu, we chose to override this facility as it can be activated from the 1-2-3 main menu anyway, which maximises the number of add-ins that can be attached to permissible function keys.

If you don't want to go through the above procedure every time you load 1-2-3, then you must attach the program in a slightly lengthier way. To do this,

1. Use the /**Worksheet, Global, Default, Other** command
2. Select the **Add-In, Set** option
3. Choose **1** as the auto-attach add-in setting
4. Select the file ALLWAYS.ADN
5. Choose **10** key, which is the APP4 (Alt+**F10**) key
6. Select **No** (or **Yes** if you want to automatically invoke the add-in whenever you start 1-2-3)
7. Select **Quit**, followed by **Update** which changes the 1-2-3 configuration file so that your instructions are obeyed.

If you have chosen **No** (for not invoking the Allways add-in automatically when starting 1-2-3), the program will enter its normal mode whenever you start it, but you can invoke Allways at any time (when in the READY mode) by simply pressing APP4 (Alt+**F10**).

If your monitor has graphics capability, Allways will provide you with a WYSIWYG display, allowing you to see all the formatting you add to your worksheet, which should resemble what you will get on paper when you print it. If, on the other hand, your monitor does not support graphics, you can still use Allways to improve your printed work.

The Allways Commands:
When Allways is activated, by pressing Alt+**F10** when 1-2-3 is in READY mode (assuming you have followed the suggestions made above) , the screen changes to its graphics mode (if your monitor supports it), and the mode indicator changes to ALLWAYS (for other mode indicators see Appendix A).

Pressing the slash (/) key, invokes the Allways menu and the mode indicator changes to MENU. From here, you can return to the 1-2-3 READY mode by either selecting **Quit**, or pressing the <Esc> key twice; once to return from the MENU mode to the ALLWAYS mode, and once more to return from the ALLWAYS mode to the 1-2-3 READY mode.

The screen dump below, shows the top-half of the screen when the Allways menu screen is displayed.

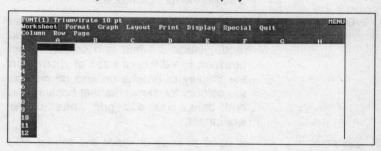

There are seven commands in the main Allways menu which can be used to enhance what Lotus 1-2-3 displays, or prints. What these commands can achieve, are listed below in the order they appear on the menu.

Command	*Function*
/Worksheet	is used to control the width of a column or a range of columns, the height of a row manually or automatically based on the font size, and page breaks.
/Format	is used to format worksheet data in any of eight fonts, add text enhancements such as bold, or underline, select a different colour for a range, add a variety of horizontal and vertical lines to a range, and shade a range.
/Graph	is used to place a .PIC graph anywhere in a worksheet, and then enhance it by changing its settings, the fonts of its text and its size and colour.

/Layout	is used to specify the appearance of the printed page by allowing you to control page size, margins, headers and footers, printer borders, and grid lines.
/Print	is used to print a specified range, send print output to a file on disc, specify the current printer and printer interface, and change the font cartridges.
/Display	is used to customise the screen display by selecting between graphics and text mode, black & white and colour, select between five different sizes of zoom, turn the display of graphs on and off choose the colours for the worksheet background and data, and add grid lines to the worksheet.
/Special	is used to copy or move the format of a range to another range, import the format and/or settings of another worksheet to the current file.

As you start using Allways to format worksheets, you might find it easier to use the Allways accelerator and function keys. These can be used as command shortcuts, reducing the number of key-strokes required for commonly used commands.

Allways Accelerator Keys:
Accelerator keys are combinations of the Alt key and a letter or number key. The letter accelerator keys cycle between one or more formats shown in parentheses. The accelerator keys are listed below:

Key-stroke	Function
Alt+B	Boldface (Set/Clear)
Alt+G	Gridlines (On/Off)
Alt+L	Lines (Outline/All/None)
Alt+S	Shading (Light/Dark/Solid/None)
Alt+U	Underline (Single/Double/None)
Alt+1	Set Font 1
Alt+2	Set Font 2

Alt+3	Set Font 3
Alt+4	Set Font 4
Alt+5	Set Font 5
Alt+6	Set Font 6
Alt+7	Set Font 7
Alt+8	Set Font 8

Allways Function Keys:

Allways uses function keys (either alone or in combination with the Alt key), some of which execute the same task as those in 1-2-3. The Allways function keys are listed below:

Key	Name	Function
F1	HELP	Displays a help screen
F3	NAME	POINT mode: Displays named ranges FILES mode: Displays file names
F4	REDUCE	Used repeatedly can reduce cells down to 60% of their normal size
F5	GOTO	Moves cell pointer to specified cell or named range
F6	DISPLAY	Switches screen display mode between graphics and text
F10	GRAPH	Turns on graph display so that graphs can be seen on screen, otherwise it only displays a hatched box within the range
Alt+F4	ENLARGE	Used repeatedly can enlarge cells up to 140% of their normal size.

Adding a Graph to a Worksheet Using Allways:

To add a graph to your current worksheet (you should have PROJECT9 on your screen), invoke Allways, move to cell location A22 and use the /Graph, Add command and specify the YEARCOST file as the .PIC file to be added to your worksheet within the range A22..F41, as shown on the next page.

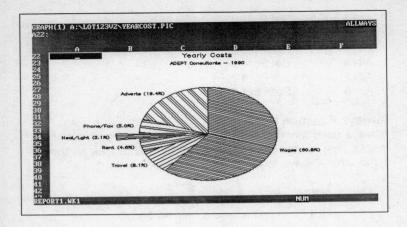

This worksheet will be used to illustrate some of the capabilities of Allways. First, we will print the worksheet range A1..F41, in a report form as it stands. Then, we will format and enhance the actual worksheet data layout, step by step, each time printing a more enhanced report, in order to cover as many Allways enhancing commands as possible.

Now use the /**Print, Range, Set** command and specify cell range A1..F44, followed by the /**Layout, Page-Size** command and choose option **1 Standard** for the paper size, followed by the **Margins** option to set the top and bottom margin to 0.5", followed by the **Titles, Header** option, and typing the words 'Income & Expenditure Report', followed by the **Footer** option, and typing the text 'December 1990||Page#'.

The print definition page should now look as follows:

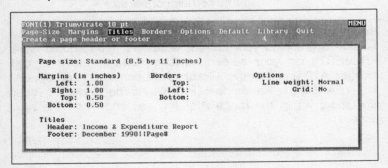

Finally, you can print your work on paper by selecting the **Go** command. The printout is shown below:

Income & Expenditure Report

ADEPT CONSULTANTS LTD
PROJECT ANALYSIS – 1990 SUMMARY

	1st Quart	2nd Quart	3rd Quart	4th Quart	TOTAL
=========	=========	=========	=========	=========	=========
Consult:	£45,000	£48,000	£49,500	£60,000	£202,500
=========	=========	=========	=========	=========	=========
Costs:					
Wages	£9,000	£12,000	£12,500	£14,000	£47,500
Travel	£1,500	£1,630	£1,400	£1,800	£6,330
Rent	£900	£900	£900	£900	£3,600
Heat/Lght	£500	£370	£230	£540	£1,640
Phone/Fax	£900	£1,050	£750	£1,230	£3,930
Adverts	£3,600	£3,900	£3,400	£4,250	£15,150
------------	------------	------------	------------	------------	------------
Tot Costs	£16,400	£19,850	£19,180	£22,720	£78,150
=========	=========	=========	=========	=========	=========
Profit	£28,600	£28,150	£30,320	£37,280	£124,350
=========	=========	=========	=========	=========	=========

Yearly Costs
ADEPT Consultants – 1990

Adverts (19.4%)
Phone/Fax (5.0%)
Heat/Lght (2.1%)
Rent (4.6%)
Wages (60.8%)
Travel (8.1%)

December 1990

Note the four special characters that can be used to format printed information. The vertical bar (|) is used to separate left-aligned, centred, and right-aligned portions of a header or footer, the hash sign (#) indicates a page number, the 'at' sign (@) indicates the current date, and the backslash (\) followed by a cell address can be used to copy cell contents to the header or footer.

Obviously, before this report becomes acceptable we need to improve the layout of the worksheet data. Another area that might need attention is the default type styles available with the Allways add-in which might not be available to your printer. However, before we start doing so, save the current worksheet under the filename REPORT1A.

The Allways Type Styles:

You can access the Allways font set with the /**Format, Font** command. The eight fonts include Triumvirate typeface in 10, 14, and 20 point size (selected with font options 1 to 4 with option 3 being in italic 10), and Times typeface in 10, 14, and 20 point size (selected with font options 5 to 8 with option 6 being in italic 10). These fonts can be replaced by using the /**Format, Font, Replace** command, which allows you to replace any of the default fonts (1-8) with a typeface of your choice from **Boldface** and **Courier**, or a library of soft fonts, if you happen to have purchased them from a third party.

As an illustration of the above points, we show overleaf the output obtained by using a Boldface 10 Printer font (using the /**Format, Font, Replace** command) to format the worksheet table on an IBM Quietwriter III printer. The result, shown overleaf, can easily be seen to be far superior to the one obtained earlier when the default Triumvirate font was used to print the same worksheet range. In fact, there has even been an improvement in the printing of the pie chart, which now is less oval than before.

However, before Allways would print out the range of the worksheet which holds the pie chart, we had to disable 1-2-3's UNDO function (using the /**Worksheet, Global, Default, Other, Undo, Disable** command), otherwise Allways reported an 'out-of-memory' error.

ADEPT CONSULTANTS LTD
PROJECT ANALYSIS - 1990 SUMMARY

	1st Quart	2nd Quart	3rd Quart	4th Quart	TOTAL
Consult:	£45,000	£48,000	£49,500	£60,000	£202,500
Costs:					
Wages	£9,000	£12,000	£12,500	£14,000	£47,500
Travel	£1,500	£1,630	£1,400	£1,800	£6,330
Rent	£900	£900	£900	£900	£3,600
Heat/Lght	£500	£370	£230	£540	£1,640
Phone/Fax	£900	£1,050	£750	£1,230	£3,930
Adverts	£3,600	£3,900	£3,400	£4,250	£15,150
Tot Costs	£16,400	£19,850	£19,180	£22,720	£78,150
Profit	£28,600	£28,150	£30,320	£37,280	£124,350

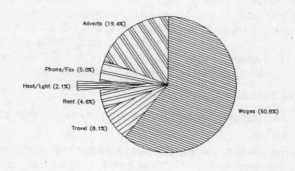

Yearly Costs
ADEPT Consultants — 1990

Adverts (19.4%)
Phone/Fax (5.0%)
Heat/Lght (2.1%)
Rent (4.6%)
Travel (8.1%)
Wages (60.8%)

Best output results can only be obtained when using a laser printer. So, if you want to produce high-quality reports, and you have access to a laser printer (even if not connected to your computer), then use the Allways Setup Disc (as discussed in the Introduction) to install the laser printer as an additional printer to be used with Allways (even if you installed such a printer to be used with 1-2-3, you must install it again to use with Allways, as the printer drivers are not the same). Then, whenever you want to use this printer from within Allways, use the /**Print, Configuration, Printer** command to enable you to make it the current printer.

From then on, you can use the Allways /**Print, File** command, which sends print output to an encoded file on disc. Such a file can be printed on a laser printer by using the DOS command

COPY *Filename.enc*/B LPT1

on the computer connected to it, without needing the 1-2-3 program.

Formatting with Allways:
We shall now use various Allways formatting commands to improve the looks of the 1990 report on Adept Consultants Ltd.

Note: Since it will be necessary to toggle frequently between 1-2-3 and Allways, using their respective commands to accomplish the task at hand, we will distinguish between the 1-2-3 and Allways commands by preceding the 1-2-3 command with the slash (/) character and the Allways commands with the less-than (<) character, even though both the 1-2-3 and the Allways menu can be activated by either of these two keys.

We carry out the following improvements:

1. Use the /**Range, Erase** command to erase the contents of cell A1.

2. Use the <**Print, Layout, Titles, Header** command and add the text '||ADEPT Consultants Ltd' to the report header, so that the additions appear on the extreme right-hand side of the printed page.

3. Use the /**Range, Erase** command to erase the equals and minus signs appearing in rows 5, 7, 15, 17, and 19, then use the <**Worksheet, Row, Set-Height** command to set the height of each of the specified rows to 5 points. Next, use the <**Format, Underline, Double,** command to draw a double underline along the range for all the specified rows. In case you are tempted to draw a single underline along a range of empty cells, note that such an

underline will neither show on your screen, nor will it print on paper. To obtain a single line along a range, use the **<Format, Lines** command and choose one of the displayed options.

Replacing the Allways Font Set:
The next lot of improvements to the looks of the worksheet requires the substitution of part of the default font set for another set of fonts, the choice of which depends entirely on your printer. Do note, however, that you might be limited in the number of fonts you can use in a single worksheet by the actual size of memory in your printer. In what follows, the Boldface printer font has been chosen, as this is the one supported by the particular printer being used here; you might have to make a different choice. Thus, to replace a font, use the **<Format, Font, Replace** command, highlight the number of the font you wish to replace and select a replacement from the displayed list which depends on what fonts your printer supports. Note that the first printer font is the one used to print the worksheet as a whole, unless you specifically format a range to be printed by another font. Below, we show the choices made here.

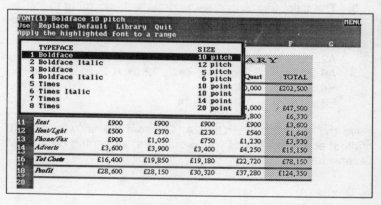

4. In order to be able to format the title of the report 'PROJECT ANALYSIS - 1990 SUMMARY' with a 5 pitch Boldface font, thus making it appear larger, you will have to shorten it somewhat, otherwise you might find that one or two of its end letters will not be printed out, even though they appear on screen. Therefore, use the 1-2-3

EDIT **(F2)** key to shorten the title to 'PROJECT ANALYSIS SUMMARY, then use the **<Format, Font, Use** command, select the required font by highlighting it and pressing <Enter>. Next, point to the range you want to format with this font and press <Enter>.

Note: A range can be highlighted before selecting a command which might prove useful when more than one enhancement is to be applied to the same range, without having to specify the range each time. For example, in order to change the font of a range, then follow it by shading the same range, first put the cell pointer in one corner of the range, press <.> to anchor it (Allways will display the ANC indicator in the status line), then use the arrow keys to highlight the required range. Do <u>not</u> press <Enter> at this point, but select the required command. On selecting a command, Allways will not prompt you for a range, but will carry out the command on the predefined range which remains highlighted until you either move the cell pointer or press <Esc>. Thus, in this way you can choose a number of commands, one after the other, applying enhancement to a range successively.

5. The following ranges were formatted according to the list below, by selecting the **<Format, Font, <Format, Bold,** or **<Format, Shade** command:

A2..F2	Boldface, 5 pitch, Shade light
A6..A19	Boldface italic, 12 pitch, Bold
B4..F4	Bold
F3..F19	Shade, light

Save the result as REPORT2A. Overleaf we show a sample printout of the top-half of your worksheet, as printed on an IBM Quietwriter III.

Income & Expenditure Report   ADEPT Consultants Ltd

PROJECT ANALYSIS SUMMARY

	1st Quart	2nd Quart	3rd Quart	4th Quart	TOTAL
Consult:	£45,000	£48,000	£49,500	£60,000	£202,500
Costs:					
Wages	£9,000	£12,000	£12,500	£14,000	£47,500
Travel	£1,500	£1,630	£1,400	£1,800	£6,330
Rent	£900	£900	£900	£900	£3,600
Heat/Lght	£500	£370	£230	£540	£1,640
Phone/Fax	£900	£1,050	£750	£1,230	£3,930
Adverts	£3,600	£3,900	£3,400	£4,250	£15,150
Tot Costs	£16,400	£19,850	£19,180	£22,720	£78,150
Profit	£28,600	£28,150	£30,320	£37,280	£124,350

Enhancing a Chart with Allways:

Allways can be used to enhance the appearance of graphs and charts. As graphs are normally transparent, if you place a graph on a part of the worksheet which holds data, the data will show through the graph. If this is not what you want to see, then add shading to the range where the graph has been placed so that it appears against a shaded background. However, data will still show through to some extent, therefore place your graphs in a range which is free of data.

One of the most versatile options of <Graph is **Settings.** With this option you can select the colours for graph data ranges, set the fonts to use for text in graphs, set the margins for the graphs, change the scaling factor for fonts, move the graph to a different range or change its size, and even replace a graph in the worksheet with a different graph by substituting a different .PIC file. What you cannot do is add explanatory text to graphs, arrows or free-hand drawings.

To illustrate the superiority of output from a laser printer, we show on the next page the full printout of our report. This was first printed to disc on an encoded file, as described earlier, then printed on an HP LaserJet II attached to a computer without any further use of 1-2-3.

On changing the current printer with the **<Print, Configuration, Printer** command, the first four fonts which were replaced earlier with Boldface-type style were automatically changed to their equivalent Times-type styles. The result is shown below:

Output on an HP LaserJet II

Income & Expenditure Report   ADEPT Consultants Ltd

PROJECT ANALYSIS SUMMARY

	1st Quart	2nd Quart	3rd Quart	4th Quart	TOTAL
Consult:	£45,000	£48,000	£49,500	£60,000	£202,500
Costs:					
Wages	£9,000	£12,000	£12,500	£14,000	£47,500
Travel	£1,500	£1,630	£1,400	£1,800	£6,330
Rent	£900	£900	£900	£900	£3,600
Heat/Lght	£500	£370	£230	£540	£1,640
Phone/Fax	£900	£1,050	£750	£1,230	£3,930
Adverts	£3,600	£3,900	£3,400	£4,250	£15,150
Tot Costs	£16,400	£19,850	£19,180	£22,720	£78,150
Profit	£28,600	£28,150	£30,320	£37,280	£124,350

Yearly Costs
ADEPT Consultants – 1990

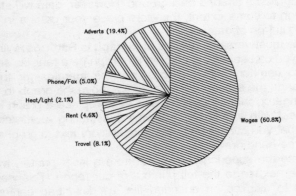

Adverts (19.4%)
Phone/Fax (5.0%)
Heat/Lght (2.1%)
Rent (4.6%)
Travel (8.1%)
Wages (60.8%)

December 1990   Page1

Removing Allways from Memory:
Allways can be removed from memory by selecting the **/Add-In** command from the main 1-2-3 menu and choosing the **Detach** option. However, before removing Allways from memory make sure you have saved your work with the **/File, Save** command, otherwise all formatting information will be lost.

In addition, make sure that Allways is attached whenever you make any changes to your worksheet, because if Allways is detached while you carry out changes to a formatting worksheet, a mismatch may occur between the cells of your worksheet and their Allways formats. The result will most certainly be confusing, as formats applied in one range might appear to influence another range.

The Wysiwyg Module - Release 2.3
To load the Wysiwyg module that comes with Lotus 1-2-3 Release 2.3 into memory, load 1-2-3 and, when the program displays a blank worksheet and is in the READY mode, then

1. Press ADDIN (Alt+**F10**)
2. Select **Attach**
3. Choose WYSIWYG.ADN
4. Select **No-Key**
5. Select **Invoke**
6. Choose WYSIWYG
7. Select **Quit**.

This way of loading Wysiwyg into memory, as opposed to assigning it to one of the APP1 to APP3 (Alt+**F7** to Alt+**F9**) keys, allows you to use the colon (:) method for accessing the Wysiwyg menu. If you want Wysiwyg to load automatically whenever you load 1-2-3, then

1. Select **/Worksheet, Global, Default**

which causes the 'Default Settings' dialogue box to be displayed,

2. Press **F2** (EDIT) function key, or click the Auto-attach add-ins field of the dialogue box, and press <Enter>
3. Type in the entry box 1:[........] WYSIWYG as the add-in you want to attach and press <Enter>
4. Press the **Update** button.

Next time you load 1-2-3, Wysiwyg will be loaded automatically into memory, and invoked.

Selecting Wysiwyg Commands:
When Wysiwyg is active, the main Lotus 1-2-3 menu can be activated by pressing the slash (/) key. You can invoke the Wysiwyg menu, either by pressing the colon (:) key on the keyboard (if you have loaded the program with the **No-Key** option), then selecting commands by typing their first letter, or by using the mouse, provided you have installed one first.

To invoke the main Lotus 1-2-3 menu with the mouse, simply move the mouse pointer into the control panel at the top of the screen. Pressing the right mouse button, toggles the menu between the main menu and the Wysiwyg menu. Selecting commands with the use of the mouse, from either menu, is a matter of pointing to a chosen command and pressing the left mouse button. Once a command has been chosen, pressing the right mouse button has the same effect as pressing <Esc> on the keyboard.

If you are a left-handed person and wish to switch the mouse buttons around so that the left button is used for the right (and vice versa), then use the Install program and select the Wysiwyg options. Other options can be used to generate fonts for printing and screen display, or add soft fonts from a disc to use with Wysiwyg.

The screen dump below, shows the top-half of the screen when the Wysiwyg menu is displayed.

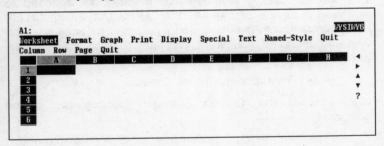

Mouse Shortcuts in Wysiwyg:
The five icons on the right hand side of the display can be used with the mouse to move the cell pointer left, right, up, or down in the current worksheet, or invoke the help screen.

76

Furthermore, you can use the mouse to create vertical or horizontal windows by pointing to the box located above row1 and to the left of column A, pressing the left mouse button and dragging the mouse to the right or down, respectively, until the desired window size is reached, then releasing the mouse button. To clear such windows, move the mouse pointer to the box above row1 of the added window and drag the mouse left or up to move the box to its original position.

Finally, you can use the mouse to specify worksheet ranges when asked by the program. You can even specify a range before selecting a command which can prove useful when trying to apply a variety of formats to a range without having to specify the range for each command. These can be achieved as follows:

- For highlighting a range after selecting a command - move the mouse pointer to one corner of the range, click the left mouse button and drag the mouse to the opposite corner of the cell range, then release the mouse button to specify the highlighted range.

- For highlighting a range prior to selecting a command - move the mouse pointer to one corner of the range, click the left mouse button and drag the mouse to the opposite corner of the cell range, then release the mouse button to specify the highlighted range. Selecting the command you want to use, causes 1-2-3 to carry out the command without asking for the range. The specified range remains highlighted (unless you move the cell pointer, press <Esc>, or click the left mouse button) ready for selecting the next command. When you have finished with all the commands you intend to apply to the highlighted range, click the left mouse button.

The Wysiwyg Commands:

There are eight commands in the main Wysiwyg menu which can be used to enhance what Lotus 1-2-3 displays, or prints. What these commands can achieve, are listed below in the order they appear on the main Wysiwyg menu.

:**Worksheet** is used to control the width of a column or a range of columns, the height of a row or a range of rows, and to insert or remove a page break.

:Format is used to format worksheet data in any of eight fonts, add text enhancements such as bold, italics, or underline, select a different colour for a range, add a variety of horizontal and vertical lines to a range, including drop shadows, and shade a range.

:Graph is used to place 1-2-3 graphs anywhere in a worksheet, and then enhance them with colours, text, arrows, and geometric shapes. You can even view and add external graph files saved under the .PIC and .CGM formats, or create free-hand drawings and annotations.

:Print is used to specify the printer, interface and font cartridges, orientation and resolution of the output, paper type and size, margins, titles, headers, footers and preview a printed range on screen.

:Display is used to customise the screen display by selecting between graphics and text mode, black & white and colour, selecting between six different sizes of zoom, choosing the colours for the worksheet background and data, specifying the cell pointer style between solid or outline, and adding grid lines to the worksheet.

:Special is used to copy or move the format of a range to another range, import the format and/or settings of another worksheet to the current file, and export formatting information to disc in a .FM3, .FMT, or .ALL file format.

:Text is used to enter information in a worksheet as if you were using a word processor. Data can be entered directly in a range (instead of in the control panel) with word wrap, font and formatting control. Text alignment is within the specified range (instead of within cells).

:Named-Style is used to assign names to groups of formats by defining up to eight such groups, so that you can later format easily and consistently other worksheet ranges with the same group of formats.

Adding a Graph to a Worksheet Using Wysiwyg:
To add a graph to your current worksheet (you should have PROJECT9 on your screen), invoke Wysiwyg, move to cell

location A22 and use the **:Graph, Add** command and specify the YEARCOST file as the .PIC file to be added to your worksheet within the range A22..F41. The result should be similar to the screen dump shown below:

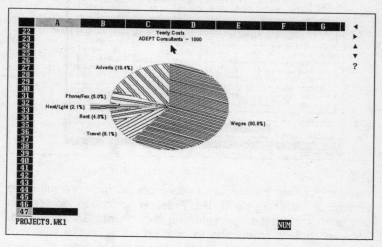

This worksheet will be used to illustrate some of the capabilities of Wysiwyg. First, we will print the worksheet range A1..F41, in a report form as it stands. Then, we will format and enhance the actual worksheet data layout, step by step, each time printing a more enhanced report, in order to cover as many Wysiwyg enhancing commands as possible.

Now use the **:Print, Range, Set** command and specify cell range A1..F44, followed by the **Layout, Page-Size** command and choose option **2:A4** for the paper size, followed by the **Titles, Header** option, and typing the words 'Income & Expenditure Report', followed by the **Footer** option, and typing the text 'December 1990||Page#'. The Print Settings screen is shown on the next page.

There are four special characters that can be used to format printed information. The vertical bar (|) is used to separate left-aligned, centred, and right-aligned portions of a header or footer, the hash sign (#) indicates a page number, the 'at' sign (@) indicates the current date, and the backslash (\) followed by a cell address can be used to copy cell contents to the header or footer.

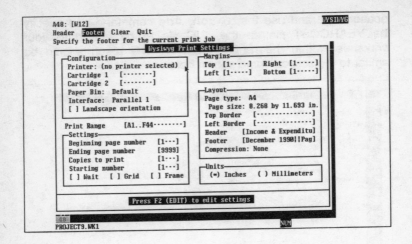

```
A48: [W12]                                                    WYSIWYG
Header  Footer  Clear  Quit
Specify the footer for the current print job
                         Wysiwyg Print Settings
   ┌Configuration─────────────────┐  ┌Margins──────────────────┐
    Printer: (no printer selected)    Top  [1·····]  Right  [1·····]
    Cartridge 1  [·········]           Left [1·····]  Bottom [1·····]
    Cartridge 2  [·········]
    Paper Bin:  Default               ┌Layout───────────────────┐
    Interface:  Parallel 1             Page type:  A4
    [ ] Landscape orientation          Page size: 8.268 by 11.693 in.
                                       Top Border   [················]
   Print Range    [A1..F44·········]   Left Border  [················]
   ┌Settings──────────────────────┐   Header   [Income & Expenditu]
    Beginning page number  [1···]      Footer   [December 1990!¦Pag]
    Ending page number     [9999]      Compression: None
    Copies to print        [1···]
    Starting number        [1···]     ┌Units────────────────────┐
    [ ] Wait  [ ] Grid  [ ] Frame      (•) Inches  ( ) Millimeters

              ┌────────────────────────────────────────┐
              │   Press F2 (EDIT) to edit settings      │
              └────────────────────────────────────────┘
   48
PROJECT9.WK1                                                   NUM
```

You can preview the layout of your work so far, on a full page display, by selecting the :**Print, Preview** command, and/or you can print it on paper by selecting the :**Print, Go** command. However, before attempting to print on paper, make sure that you have used the :**Print, Config** command in order to select the appropriate printer driver. Also make sure that the whole of the selected range of the current worksheet fits on a single report page. If not, use the /**Worksheet, Column, Column-Range, Set-Width** command to set range A1..F1 to a width of 9 characters. The printout is shown on the next page.

Obviously, before this report becomes acceptable we need to use quite a bit of cosmetic surgery, particularly on the layout of the worksheet data. Another area that needs attention is the default type styles available with Wysiwyg which might not be available to your printer. However, before we start doing so, save the current worksheet under the filename REPORT1W.

The Wysiwyg Type Styles:
You can access the Wysiwyg font set with the :**Format, Font** command. The eight fonts include Swiss typeface in 12, 14, and 24 point size (selected with font options 1 to 3), Dutch typeface in 6, 8, 10, and 12 point size (selected with font options 4 to 7), and Xsymbol typeface in 12 point size (selected with font option 8). These fonts can be replaced by using the :**Format, Font, Replace** command, which allows you to replace any of the

default fonts (1-8) with a typeface of your choice from **Swiss, Dutch, Courier, Xsymbol,** and **Other** (with the latter including a list of 18, mainly fonts used with a PostScript printer), with point sizes ranging from 3 to 72. However, you should only select those fonts which are supported by your printer.

Income & Expenditure Report

ADEPT CONSULTANTS LTD
PROJECT ANALYSIS – 1990 SUMMARY

	1st Quart	2nd Quart	3rd Quart	4th Quart	TOTAL
Consult:	£45,000	£48,000	£49,500	£60,000	£202,500
Costs:					
Wages	£9,000	£12,000	£12,500	£14,000	£47,500
Travel	£1,500	£1,630	£1,400	£1,800	£6,330
Rent	£900	£900	£900	£900	£3,600
Heat/Lght	£500	£370	£230	£540	£1,640
Phone/Fax	£900	£1,050	£750	£1,230	£3,930
Adverts	£3,600	£3,900	£3,400	£4,250	£15,150
Tot Costs	£16,400	£19,850	£19,180	£22,720	£78,150
Profit	£28,600	£28,150	£30,320	£37,280	£124,350

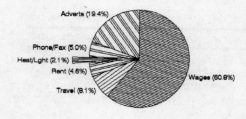

Yearly Costs
ADEPT Consultants – 1990

Adverts (19.4%)
Phone/Fax (5.0%)
Heat/Lght (2.1%)
Rent (4.6%)
Travel (8.1%)
Wages (60.8%)

Even if you choose the correct character fonts for your printer, 1-2-3 will use your printer's graphics capability to print your work when you select the **:Print, Go** command producing an inferior output. If, however, you select the **/Print, Printer, Go** command (you will have to specify the **Range** again), the output will be at its best for your particular printer, but since it was printed in text form, the graph in the included range will not be printed. As an illustration of these points, we show below the output obtained by using a Courier 12 to format the worksheet table on an IBM Quietwriter III printer. The first half of the output was produced by printing in graphics mode, while the second half was produced by printing in text mode.

```
ADEPT CONSULTANTS LTD
PROJECT ANALYSIS - 1990 SUMMARY

          1st Quart2nd Quart3rd Quart4th Quart    TOTAL
=========================================================
Consult:  £45,000  £48,000  £49,500  £60,000 £202,500
=========================================================
Costs:
Wages      £9,000  £12,000  £12,500  £14,000  £47,500
Travel     £1,500   £1,630   £1,400   £1,800   £6,330
Rent         £900     £900     £900     £900   £3,600
Heat/Lght    £500     £370     £230     £540   £1,640
Phone/Fax    £900   £1,050     £750   £1,230   £3,930
Adverts    £3,600   £3,900   £3,400   £4,250  £15,150
---------------------------------------------------------
Tot Costs £16,400  £19,850  £19,180  £22,720  £78,150
=========================================================
Profit    £28,600  £28,150  £30,320  £37,280 £124,350
=========================================================
```

```
ADEPT CONSULTANTS LTD
PROJECT ANALYSIS - 1990 SUMMARY

          1st Quart2nd Quart3rd Quart4th Quart    TOTAL
=========================================================
Consult:  £45,000  £48,000  £49,500  £60,000 £202,500
=========================================================
Costs:
Wages      £9,000  £12,000  £12,500  £14,000  £47,500
Travel     £1,500   £1,630   £1,400   £1,800   £6,330
Rent         £900     £900     £900     £900   £3,600
Heat/Lght    £500     £370     £230     £540   £1,640
Phone/Fax    £900   £1,050     £750   £1,230   £3,930
Adverts    £3,600   £3,900   £3,400   £4,250  £15,150
---------------------------------------------------------
Tot Costs £16,400  £19,850  £19,180  £22,720  £78,150
=========================================================
Profit    £28,600  £28,150  £30,320  £37,280 £124,350
=========================================================
```

Best output results can only be obtained when using a laser printer with PostScript capability. So, if you want to produce high-quality reports, and you have access to a PostScript printer, then use the Install program to install it as a second printer, then select the **:Print, Config, Printer** command to make it the current printer. From then on, use the **:Print, File** command which sends print output to an encoded file on disc. Such a file can be printed on your laser printer by using the DOS command

COPY *Filename.Ext*/B LPT1

on the computer connected to it, without needing the 1-2-3 program.

Wysiwyg Formatting:
We shall now use various Wysiwyg formatting commands to improve the looks of the 1990 report on Adept Consultants Ltd. We carry out the following improvements:

1. Delete row 1 of the worksheet by using the **/Worksheet, Delete** command.

2. Add the text '||ADEPT Consultants Ltd' to the report header, using the **:Print, Layout, Titles, Header** command so that the additions appear on the extreme right-hand side of the printed page.

3. Replace the equals and minus signs now appearing in rows 4, 6, 14, 16, and 18, by first erasing the contents of each of the specified rows using the **/Range, Erase** command, then use the **:Worksheet, Row, Set-Height** command to set the height of each of the specified rows to 5 points. Next, use the **:Format, Lines, Double, Top** command to draw double horizontal lines at the top edge of each cell in the range for all the specified rows, except row 14. For row 14 use a single horizontal line at the top edge of each cell in the required range.

4. Centre the report title (in A1) by using the **:Text, Align, Center** command and specifying A1..F1 as the range within which it is to be aligned. Next, use the **:Text, Set** command to set the range to be used with the **:Text, Edit**

option, press <Enter> to accept the displayed edit range and press NAME (**F3**) to reveal a sub-menu from which choose **Italics**, followed by **F3**, **Outline**, and pressing <Esc> to finish.

Save the result as REPORT2W. The top-half of your worksheet should now look as follows:

```
A1: {Text} [W12] ^▲i▲oPROJECT ANALYSIS - 1990 SUMMARY                    WYSIWYG
Worksheet  Format  Graph  Print  Display  Special  Text  Named-Style  Quit
Go  File  Background  Range  Config  Settings  Layout  Preview  Info  Quit
```

	A	B	C	D	E	F
1		*PROJECT ANALYSIS - 1990 SUMMARY*				
2						
3		1st Quart	2nd Quart	3rd Quart	4th Quart	TOTAL
5	Consult:	£45,000	£48,000	£49,500	£60,000	£202,500
7	Costs:					
8	Wages	£9,000	£12,000	£12,500	£14,000	£47,500
9	Travel	£1,500	£1,630	£1,400	£1,800	£6,330
10	Rent	£900	£900	£900	£900	£3,600
11	Heat/Lght	£500	£370	£230	£540	£1,640
12	Phone/Fax	£900	£1,050	£750	£1,230	£3,930
13	Adverts	£3,600	£3,900	£3,400	£4,250	£15,150
15	Tot Costs	£16,400	£19,850	£19,180	£22,720	£78,150
17	Profit	£28,600	£28,150	£30,320	£37,280	£124,350
19						

5. Remove the graph from the display by using the **:Graph, Remove** command, then remove the second line of the graph title by using the **/Graph, Options, Titles, Second** command, backspacing to delete the displayed text and pressing <Enter>, then use **/Graph, Options, Titles, First** command and change the chart title from 'Yearly Costs' to 'COSTS PROJECTIONS. Next, use the **:Graph, Add, Current** command to re-insert the edited pie chart in range A21..F40.

6. Add text to the graph portion of the display by first using the **:Graph, Goto** command and select <CURRENT>, which moves the cell pointer to the beginning of the graph area (in this case A21). Next, select the **:Graph, Edit** command, specifying the graphic to edit as A21 by pressing <Enter>, choosing the **Add, Text** option and typing the text 'For the Year 1990'. Use the arrow keys to place the text in the graph, centrally positioned, under its

main caption, then use the options **Add, Line** and **Add, Arrow** to add a horizontal line and an inclined arrow.

Save the result as REPORT3W. The bottom-half of your worksheet should now look as follows:

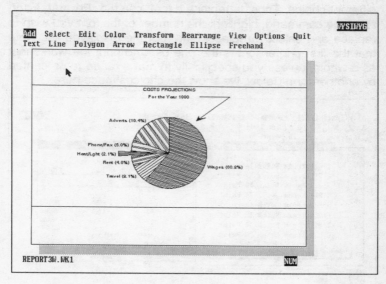

Note: Objects within a graphic window (which can be a line of text, a geometric shape, or a free-hand drawing) that you have added with the **:Graph, Edit** commands, can be edited, moved or removed. However, before you can carry out any of these commands, you must 'select', or identify such objects using the **:Graph, Edit, Select** command (or when using the mouse, by pointing to the required object and double clicking the left mouse button). When an object has been selected, small filled squares appear on its outer edges. You can move such objects by pointing to one of the small filled squares and dragging them to a new position.

Replacing the Wysiywg Font Set:
The next lot of improvements to the looks of the worksheet requires the substitution of part of the default font set for another set of fonts, the choice of which depends entirely on

your printer. Do note, however, that you might be limited in the number of fonts you can use in a single worksheet by the actual size of memory in your printer.

In what follows, the Swiss printer font has been chosen, as an example of how to replace fonts; you might have to make a different choice. Thus, to replace a font, use the **:Format, Font, Replace** command, highlight the number of the font you wish to replace and select a replacement from the displayed list. Note that the first printer font is the one used to print the worksheet as a whole, unless you specifically format a range to be printed by another font. Below, we show the choices made here.

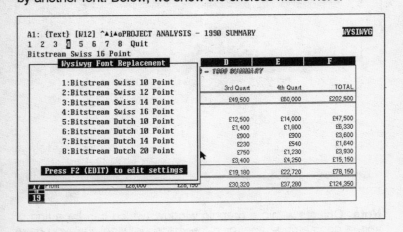

7. In order to be able to format the title of the report 'PROJECT ANALYSIS - 1990 SUMMARY' with a 16 point Swiss font, thus making it appear larger, you will have to shorten it somewhat, otherwise you might find that one or two of its end letters will not be printed out, even though they appear on screen. Therefore, use the 1-2-3 EDIT (**F2**) key to shorten the title to 'PROJECT ANALYSIS SUMMARY, then use the **:Format, Font** command, select the required font by highlighting it and pressing <Enter>. Next, enter the range you want to format with this font and press <Enter>.

Note: A range can be highlighted before selecting a command which might prove useful when more than one enhancement is to be applied to the same range, without having to specify the range each time. For example, in order to change the font of a range, then follow it by shading the same range, first highlight the range by dragging the mouse. Do not press <Enter> at this point, but select the required command. On selecting a command, Wysiwyg will not prompt you for a range, but will carry out the command on the predefined range which remains highlighted until you either move the cell pointer or press <Esc>. Thus, in this way you can choose a number of commands, one after the other, applying enhancement to a range successively.

8. The following ranges were formatted according to the list below, by selecting the appropriate :**Format** options:

A1..A1	Swiss, 16 point
A5..A17	Swiss 12 point, Italic
B5..F5	Swiss 10 point, Bold
B15..F15	Swiss 10 point, Bold
B17..F17	Swiss 10 point, Bold
F3..F17	Shade, light

Save the result as REPORT4W. The final printout, using a PostScript printer, is shown on the next page. The report was first printed to disc on an encoded file, as described earlier, then printed from a computer without any further use of 1-2-3.

Removing Wysiwyg from Memory:
Wysiwyg can be removed from memory by pressing ADDIN (Alt+**F10**) and choosing the **Detach** option. However, before removing Wysiwyg from memory, make sure you have saved your work with the /**File, Save** command, otherwise all formatting information will be lost.

Output on a PostScript Printer

Income & Expenditure Report   ADEPT Consultants Ltd

PROJECT ANALYSIS SUMMARY

	1st Quart	2nd Quart	3rd Quart	4th Quart	TOTAL
Consult:	**£45,000**	**£48,000**	**£49,500**	**£60,000**	**£202,500**
Costs:					
Wages	£9,000	£12,000	£12,500	£14,000	£47,500
Travel	£1,500	£1,630	£1,400	£1,800	£6,330
Rent	£900	£900	£900	£900	£3,600
Heat/Lght	£500	£370	£230	£540	£1,640
Phone/Fax	£900	£1,050	£750	£1,230	£3,930
Adverts	£3,600	£3,900	£3,400	£4,250	£15,150
Tot Costs	**£16,400**	**£19,850**	**£19,180**	**£22,720**	**£78,150**
Profit	**£28,600**	**£28,150**	**£30,320**	**£37,280**	**£124,350**

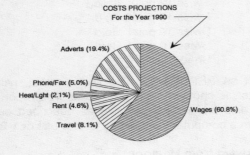

COSTS PROJECTIONS
For the Year 1990

Adverts (19.4%)
Phone/Fax (5.0%)
Heat/Lght (2.1%)
Rent (4.6%)
Travel (8.1%)
Wages (60.8%)

* * *

Both Allways and Wysiwyg have many more commands that can be use to produce more professional-looking reports. In fact, one could devote a whole book on the subject. Nevertheless, what little has been discussed here, will form a good foundation from which to explore the package(s) and add to your knowledge.

* * *

6. DATABASE MANAGEMENT

A 1-2-3 database is a worksheet range which contains related information, such as 'Customer's Names', 'Consultancy Details', 'Invoice No.' etc. A phone book is a simple database table, stored on paper. In Lotus 1-2-3 each record is entered as a worksheet row, with the fields of each record occupying corresponding columns.

A worksheet can contain many databases, each organised around a specific theme or requirement, and used for storing information so that it is quickly accessible. To make accessing the data easier, each row, or **record,** of data within a database is structured in the same fashion, i.e. each record will have the same number of columns or **fields**.

We define a database and its various elements as follows:

Database   A collection of related data organised in rows and columns in a worksheet file. A worksheet file can contain many different databases

Record   A row of information relating to a single entry and comprising of one or more fields

Field   A single column of information of the same type, such as name of customers.

Setting-up a Database

In order to investigate the various database functions, such as sorting, searching, date calculations, etc., we first need to set-up a worksheet in the form shown overleaf.

Note that in creating a database, the following rules must be observed:

1. The top row of the database must contain the field labels, one per column, which identify the fields in the database. The second and subsequent rows of such a database must contain records; no blank rows should be inserted between the field labels and the actual records.

2. Field labels must be unique within a given database.

3. Entries under each field must be of the same type.

4. A database can contain a maximum of 256 fields and 8,191 records.

We assume that the 'Invoice Analysis' of Adept Consultants is designed and set out as shown below with the listed field titles and field widths. Formatting information is given below.

```
D5: (D4) [W9] "10/4/90                                          READY

          A              B           C      D     E  F      G
1                           INVOICE ANALYSIS: ADEPT CONSULTANTS LTD  AT 26/01/91
2
3         CUSTOMER       CONSULTANCY  INUC   DATE  P/D DAYS   TOTAL
4           NAME           DETAILS     No   ISSUED Y/N OVER   VALUE
5     VORTEX Co. Ltd    Wind Tunnel Tests 9001 10/4/90  N        £120.84
6     AVON Construction Adhesive Tests    9002 22/4/90  Y        £103.52
7     BARROWS Associates Tunnel Design Tests 9003 17/5/90 N       £99.32
8     STONEAGE Ltd      Carbon Dating Tests 9004 29/5/90 N        £55.98
9     PARKWAY Gravel    Material Size Tests 9005 14/6/90 N       £180.22
10    WESTWOOD Ltd      Load Bearing Tests 9006 27/6/90  N        £68.52
11    GLOWORM Ltd       Luminescence Tests 9007  7/7/90  N       £111.55
12    SILVERSMITH Co    X-Ray Diffract. Test 9008 19/7/90 Y      £123.45
13    WORMGLAZE Ltd     Heat Transfer Tests 9009 16/8/90 N        £35.87
14    EALING Engines Dgn Vibration Tests   9010  2/9/90  N        £58.95
15    HIRE Service Equip Network Implement'n 9011 20/9/90 N      £290.00
16    EUROBASE Co. Ltd  Proj. Contr. Manag. 9012 18/10/90 N      £150.00
17    FREEMARKET Dealers Stock Control Pack. 9013 9/11/90 N      £560.00
18    OILRIG Construct.  Metal Fatigue Tests 9014 23/11/90 N      £96.63
19    TIME & Motion Ltd Systems Analysis    9015 13/12/90 N      £120.35
20    AVON Construction Cement Fatigue Tests 9016 11/1/91 N      £111.89
INVOICE1.WK1                                            NUM
```

Use the /**Worksheet, Column, Set-Width** command to change the width of the various columns to those given below, and then enter the abbreviated titles, centrally positioned, in two rows as shown in the worksheet above. These widths were chosen so that the whole of the worksheet could be seen on the screen at once.

Column	Title	Width	Type
A	CUSTOMER NAME	19	Default
B	CONSULT DETAILS	20	Default
C	INVOICE No	6	Fixed, 0 decimal
D	DATE ISSUED	9	Date, type 4
E	PAID? (Y/N)	3	Default
F	DAYS OVER	6	Fixed, 0 decimal
G	TOTAL VALUE	9	Currency, 2 decimal

Use the /**Range, Format, Fixed** command to format column C and F to 0 (zero) decimal places, and then the /**Range, Format, Currency** command to format column G to 2 decimal places, before entering information. The dates in Column D were entered with the quotes (") prefix. Column F will be calculated

92

later using a formula which relies on information held in columns D and E. However, for the time being, leave this column empty and, when you complete the other entries, save the resultant worksheet under the filename INVOICE1.

Sorting a Database

The records within the above database are in the order in which they were entered, with the 'Invoice No' shown in ascending order. However, once records have been entered, we might find it easier to browse through the information if it was sorted in alphabetical order of, say, 'Customer Name'. Lotus 1-2-3 has an easy to use sort function. To use it, place the cell pointer at the beginning of the sort range (in this case A5), then press

/	to reveal the menus
D	to select **Data**
S	to select **Sort**
D	to select **Data-Range**
<.>	to anchor beginning of sort range
<Arrows>	to highlight the sort range (A5..G20)
<Enter>	to confirm range selection
P	to select **Primary-Key**
<Enter>	to confirm primary range selection (A5)
A	to select Ascending sort order
<Enter>	to confirm selection
G	to select **Go**.

Issuing these commands, produces a sorted database under the 'Customer Name', but information under a given customer might not be in invoice order and, therefore, chronologically in the wrong order (note, for example, the invoice order of AVON Construction on your screen).

To remedy this, select the **Secondary-Key** sort field (you don't even have to confirm the sort block range or the primary sort fields, as 1-2-3 remembers these), and specify the 'Invoice No' column. If you want to reset any of these 'remembered' ranges, then choose the appropriate sort function and press <Esc> to allow re-definition of the specific choice.

With Release 2.2, as you enter information on the range to be sorted, the primary and secondary keys, and their order of sorting, the program copies and displays the information on a

'Sort Settings' screen, as shown below. This makes it a lot easier to see at a glance the choices made.

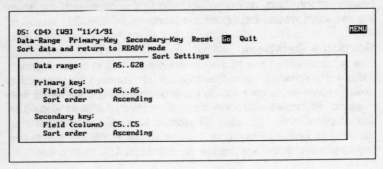

```
D5: (D4) [W9] "11/1/91                                          MENU
Data-Range Primary-Key Secondary-Key Reset Go Quit
Sort data and return to READY mode
┌───────────────────── Sort Settings ─────────────────────┐
│    Data range:        A5..G20                            │
│                                                          │
│    Primary key:                                          │
│       Field (column) A5..A5                              │
│       Sort order     Ascending                           │
│                                                          │
│    Secondary key:                                        │
│       Field (column) C5..C5                              │
│       Sort order     Ascending                           │
└──────────────────────────────────────────────────────────┘
```

With Release 2.3, a similar 'Sort Settings' dialogue box is displayed instead, but serves the same purpose.

Having defined C5 as the **Secondary-Key** sort field, selecting **Go** displays the following screen:

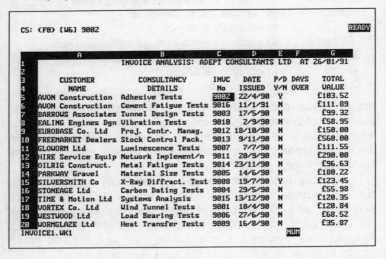

```
C5: (F0) [W6] 9002                                            READY

        A                  B            C      D     E  F      G
1                  INVOICE ANALYSIS: ADEPT CONSULTANTS LTD  AT 26/01/91
2
3      CUSTOMER          CONSULTANCY    INVC   DATE  P/D DAYS  TOTAL
4      NAME              DETAILS        No    ISSUED Y/N OVER  VALUE
5   AVON Construction Adhesive Tests    9002  22/4/90  Y      £103.52
6   AVON Construction Cement Fatigue Tests 9016 11/1/91 N    £111.89
7   BARROWS Associates Tunnel Design Tests 9003 17/5/90 N     £99.32
8   EALING Engines Dgn Vibration Tests  9010  2/9/90  N       £58.95
9   EUROBASE Co. Ltd  Proj. Contr. Manag. 9012 18/10/90 N    £150.00
10  FREEMARKET Dealers Stock Control Pack. 9013 9/11/90 N    £560.00
11  GLOWORM Ltd       Luminescence Tests 9007  7/7/90  N      £111.55
12  HIRE Service Equip Network Implement/n 9011 20/9/90 N    £290.00
13  OILRIG Construct.  Metal Fatigue Tests 9014 23/11/90 N    £96.63
14  PARKWAY Gravel    Material Size Tests 9005 14/6/90  N    £180.22
15  SILVERSMITH Co    X-Ray Diffract. Test 9008 19/7/90  Y   £123.45
16  STONEAGE Ltd      Carbon Dating Tests 9004 29/5/90  N     £55.98
17  TIME & Motion Ltd Systems Analysis  9015 13/12/90 N      £120.35
18  VORTEX Co. Ltd    Wind Tunnel Tests 9001 10/4/90  N      £120.84
19  WESTWOOD Ltd      Load Bearing Tests 9006 27/6/90  N      £68.52
20  WORMGLAZE Ltd     Heat Transfer Tests 9009 16/8/90  N     £35.87
INVOICE1.WK1                                           NUM
```

Now re-sort the database in ascending order of 'Invoice No' so that you obtain the original data entry screen display.

Using Functions in a Database

Functions can be used in a database to assist with data manipulation, for example, calculating the number of days an invoice is overdue. In addition, you can use special database functions to perform statistical calculations on information held in a database. These are listed in Appendix C.

Date Arithmetic:

There are several date functions which can be used in 1-2-3 to carry out date calculations. For example, typing the function @DATE(91,1,26) - 26/1/91 backwards, works out the number of days since 31 December 1899, while typing @NOW (as in cell G1 of the worksheet), gives the number of days (in decimal) since the beginning of the century, but using the internal clock. The decimal part has to do with time. These date numbers can only be seen if you have not used the **/Worksheet, Global, Format, Date** command. If you use this command and select option **4 (Long Intn'l)**, then the cell displays the actual date in the usual form (26/1/91).

Another function, the @DATEVALUE, allows a date entered in the declared format of the spreadsheet (such as that in cell D5 - 10/4/90) to be used in calculations. Thus, typing

@NOW-@DATEVALUE("10/4/90") or
@NOW-@DATEVALUE(D5)

gives the difference in days, if the appropriate worksheet cell is formatted for integer (Fixed, 0 decimals) numbers, between now and the mentioned date.

We will use these two functions to work out the number of overdue days of the unpaid invoices in our example, by typing in cell F5 the following formula:

@NOW-@DATEVALUE(D5)

If the record in row 5 of the worksheet refers to the data of VORTEX Co. Ltd., then the result should be 291 days, provided you are actually performing this calculation on 26/1/91, otherwise your result will differ substantially from the one discussed above. The reason for this is, of course, that the @NOW function returns different numerical values when used at different dates. To get the same results as those shown in what follows, change the contents of cell G1 to "26/01/91, then edit or re-type the formula in cell F5 to replace the @NOW function with @DATEVALUE($G$1) where $G$1 causes an 'absolute' reference to be made to the contents of cell G1. The complete formula in cell F5 should now be

@DATEVALUE($G$1)-@DATEVALUE(D5)

However, before you proceed to copy the above formula to the rest of the F column of the database data block, you should take into consideration the fact that, normally, such information is not necessary if an invoice has been paid. Therefore, you need to edit the above formula in such a way as to make the result conditional to non-payment of the issued invoice.

The @IF Function:
The @IF function allows comparison between two values with the use of a special 'logical' operators (for other operators see list under section 'Order of Priority in Formulae' in Chapter 2). The logical operators we can use are listed below.

Logical operators

=	Equal to
<	Less-than
>	Greater-than
<=	Less-than or Equal to
>=	Greater-than or Equal to
<>	Not-Equal to

The general format of the @IF function is as follows:

@IF(Comparison, Outcome-if-true, Outcome-if-false)

which contains three arguments separated by commas. The first argument is the logical comparison, the second is what should happen if the outcome of the logical comparison is 'true', while the third is what should happen if the outcome of the logical comparison is false.

Thus, we can incorporate the @IF function in the formula of cell F6 to calculate the days overdue only if the invoice has not been paid, otherwise the string 'N/A' should be written into the appropriate cell should the contents of the corresponding E column of a record be anything else but N. To edit the formula

96

in cell F5, highlight the cell and use the EDIT (**F2**) key. Then press the <Home> cursor key to place the cursor at the beginning of the existing formula in the control area at the top of the worksheet and insert

@IF(E5="N",

then press the <End> cursor key to move the cursor to the end of the existing entry and add

," N/A")

The edited formula in cell F6 should now correspond to what is shown as the contents of that cell below. Now copy this formula to the rest of the appropriate range (F6..F20) and compare your results with those shown below.

```
F5: (F0) [W6] @IF(E5="N",@DATEVALUE($G$1)-@DATEVALUE(D5)," N/A")        READY
```

	A	B	C	D	E	F	G
1		INVOICE ANALYSIS: ADEPT CONSULTANTS LTD				AT	26/01/91
2							
3	CUSTOMER	CONSULTANCY	INVC	DATE	P/D	DAYS	TOTAL
4	NAME	DETAILS	No	ISSUED	Y/N	OVER	VALUE
5	VORTEX Co. Ltd	Wind Tunnel Tests	9001	18/4/90	N	291	£120.84
6	AVON Construction	Adhesive Tests	9002	22/4/90	Y	N/A	£103.52
7	BARROWS Associates	Tunnel Design Tests	9003	17/5/90	N	254	£99.32
8	STONEAGE Ltd	Carbon Dating Tests	9004	29/5/90	N	242	£55.98
9	PARKWAY Gravel	Material Size Tests	9005	14/6/90	N	226	£180.22
10	WESTWOOD Ltd	Load Bearing Tests	9006	27/6/90	N	213	£68.52
11	GLOWORM Ltd	Luminescence Tests	9007	7/7/90	N	203	£111.55
12	SILVERSMITH Co	X-Ray Diffract. Test	9008	19/7/90	Y	N/A	£123.45
13	WORMGLAZE Ltd	Heat Transfer Tests	9009	16/8/90	N	163	£35.87
14	EALING Engines Dgn	Vibration Tests	9010	2/9/90	N	146	£58.95
15	HIRE Service Equip	Network Implement/n	9011	20/9/90	N	128	£290.00
16	EUROBASE Co. Ltd	Proj. Contr. Manag.	9012	18/10/90	N	100	£150.00
17	FREEMARKET Dealers	Stock Control Pack.	9013	9/11/90	N	78	£560.00
18	OILRIG Construct.	Metal Fatigue Tests	9014	23/11/90	N	64	£96.63
19	TIME & Motion Ltd	Systems Analysis	9015	13/12/90	N	44	£120.35
20	AVON Construction	Cement Fatigue Tests	9016	11/1/91	N	15	£111.89

```
INVOICE2.WK1                                                    NUM
```

WARNING: It is important that you enter the date, in cells which will be used later for calculations, in the format that you have specified as your replacement to the default 'Date' format of your worksheet. It should be obvious that unless the @NOW function, which uses the specified internal format for date, is of the same type as the entered dates in other cells, to which you intend to apply 'date' arithmetic, then the result of such calculations will be incorrect. If you have to change the default 'date' format, then use the /**Worksheet, Global, Default, Other, International, Date** command and choose the type preferred (option **B** in the previous example). However, make quite sure that you use the **Update** command (one level back - pressing Q once - after selecting the date type) to make such choice permanent. If you don't use the **Update** command, even if everything appears as it should be this time, when you reload your worksheet later, the fields containing the results of 'date' calculations will be filled with ERR, because the worksheet would have reverted back to its default 'date' format. If you get such errors, follow the suggestions above and don't forget to use CALC (**F9**) to recalculate the worksheet.

After making the above suggested changes to your worksheet, save the result under the filename INVOICE2.

Frequency Distribution:
A frequency distribution of data allows us to find how many values in a specified range fall within specified numeric intervals (otherwise known as the bin range).

Thus, if we want to find out how many unpaid invoices exist in our database within 0-30, 31-60, 61-90, etc., days, then we need to specify the bin range in a column of the database and allocate another column to receive the frequency values. We choose to insert two columns between the existing F and G columns of the database by highlighting column G and using the /**Worksheet, Insert, Column** command, moving the cell pointer to the right once so as to highlight the range G5..H5 and pressing <Enter>. Then, move the cell pointer to A1 and use the /**Worksheet, Titles, Vertical** command to freeze the titles of column A so they remain visible while working with columns H and I. Next, use the /**Range, Format, Fixed** command to format the ranges in the two new columns to the following:

Range	Title	Width	Type
G5..G20	BIN RANGE	6	Fixed, 0 decimals
H5..H20	FREQ DIST	4	Fixed, 0 decimals

Now enter the values you want to use as intervals for the calculation of the frequency distribution into the bin range column, in this case G5..G20, as shown in the worksheet output display below. You could use the /**Data, Fill** command to do this the easy way.

To calculate the frequency distribution, highlight cell H5 and press

/	to reveal the menus
D	to select **Data**
D	to select **Distribution**
<Left>	to highlight beginning of data range (F5)
<.>	to anchor beginning of range
<Down>	to highlight range (F5..F20)
<Enter>	to confirm highlighted area
<Left>	to highlight beginning of bin range (G5)
<.>	to anchor beginning of range
<Down>	to highlight range (G5..G20)
<Enter>	to confirm highlighted area

The result of the frequency distribution is shown below.

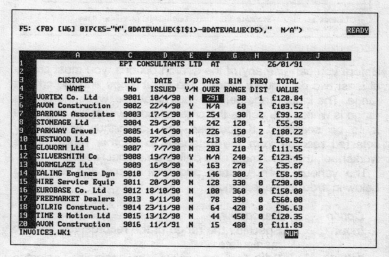

From the frequency distribution display it can be seen that there is 1 invoice within the period 0-30 days, 1 invoice within the period 31-60 days, 2 between 61-90, 1 between 91-120, etc. Save this worksheet under the filename INVOICE3.

Searching a Database

A database can be searched for specific records that meet the criteria established by the use of the **/Data, Query** command. We will use the database of worksheet INVOICE3 to illustrate the method by searching the database with the criterion relating to the frequency distribution of invoices.

Assuming that the database is on your screen, select the **/Data, Query** command, which causes the following 'Query Settings' screen to be displayed:

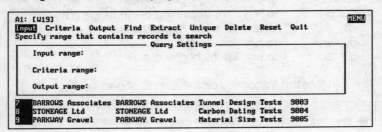

Before you can use any of the search options, you must create at least two data query ranges; the input range and the criteria range. The input range defines your database, while the criteria range is where you define the criteria under which the database is to be searched. If you use any commands which copy selected records from the database to another range in the worksheet, then you must also define an output range.

The various query options and their description are listed below in order of appearance.

Option	Description
Input	Specifies the range of the records you want to manipulate
Criteria	Specifies the range that contains selected criteria for searching or manipulating a database input range
Output	Specifies the range where you want the results of a query by the Extract or Unique option to be placed
Find	Locates and highlights the records in the input range that match the criteria in the criteria range

Extract	Copies to the output range those records from the input range that match the criteria specified in the criteria range
Unique	Copies to the output range those unique records (omits duplicate records) from the input range that match the criteria specified in the criteria range
Delete	Deletes the records in the input range that match the criteria in the criteria range
Reset	Clears the settings for the input, criteria, and output ranges.

To illustrate how some of these options work, first use the **/Worksheet, Titles, Clear** command to unfreeze any columns or rows so that you can use the cursor keys to point to the entire database range, then specify the input range of the data, using the **/Data, Query, Input** command, which must include the field names (in our example this range is A4..I20).

Next, set-up two more ranges in the worksheet, one for specifying the criteria for the search, and the other for copying records extracted from the database (the latter is only needed if the **Extract** or **Unique** options are used). To do this, first copy some or all of the field names of the database (we will choose to copy all of them) to an empty area of the worksheet, say, K4..S4 which will form the first line of the 'criteria range' and label this area CRITERIA RANGE in cell K2. Then, copy again the same field names to K12..S20 and label that area OUTPUT RANGE in cell K10.

Finally, set the width of the cells and format them according to the table below which correspond to those of the database.

Column	Field	Width	Type
K	NAME	W19	Default
L	DETAILS	W20	Default
M	No	W6	F0
N	ISSUED	W9	D4
O	Y/N	W3	Default
P	OVER	W6	F0
Q	RANGE	W6	Default
R	DIST	W4	Default
S	VALUE	W9	C2

Save the resultant worksheet under the filename INVOICE4. The criteria and output ranges are shown below:

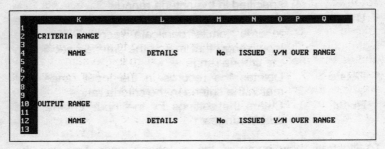

Finding and Deleting Records:

To search the database for all the details of our customers whose invoices fall within a Bin Range of 80 or more days, but whose frequency distribution is greater than 0, we need to type in cell Q5 the criterion +G5>=80 and in cell R5 the criterion +H5>0, where G5 and H5 are the appropriate fields of the first record of the database data.

In general, criteria must be entered in the second and subsequent rows of the criterion range, with each criterion entered below the copy of the appropriate field name. A label or a value may be entered exactly as it appears in the database or the two special characters ? and * can be used to match any single character of a label or all characters to the end of the label. Preceding a label with a tilde (~), causes the search of all labels except for that one. Thus, ~Y* searches the database for all records with an entry in that field which does not begin with Y.

Thus, to search a database for values, either enter the value as the exact criterion or use a formula, such as +G5>=80 in which the logical operators (<, <=, >, >=, <>) can be used. The logical formula generates a value of 1 if the condition is TRUE or a value of 0 if the condition is FALSE. This value appears in the criterion range, unless the specific cell containing the formula is formatted as 'text', using the /**Range, Format, Text** command in which case the actual formula (or part thereof - depending on the width of the cell) will appear in the corresponding criterion cell.

Several criteria can be entered, either in the same row, if you want 1-2-3 to search for records that match every criterion (i.e. criteria entered are linked with the logical AND), or one per row, if you want 1-2-3 to search records that satisfy any of the criteria (i.e. criteria entered are linked with the logical OR). Compounded logical formulas can be used to create compound criteria that match more than one condition in the same field by using #AND#, #OR# or #NOT# in the formula. For example, if we type the criterion in Q5 as +G5>=80#AND#+G5<330 and erased that in R3 (unwanted criteria must be erased rather than over-typed with a space), we would retrieve the same records that will be retrieved by the use of the two separate criteria, discussed previously.

Finally, before we can search a database, we need to specify the criterion range, which must include the field names and at least one following row in which the criteria for the search appear (in our example K4..S5), via the /Data, Query, Criterion command. Criteria may be included that refer to one field or to several (up to 32) fields of the database. Do not specify an empty line as part of the criterion range, as this has the effect of searching the database for all records.

To search the database for the criteria discussed above, use the /Data, Query, Find command which causes 1-2-3 to highlight the first record that matches the criteria which in this case is that of Tunnel BARROWS Associates. Pressing the down arrow key finds the next record that matches the chosen criteria. If there are no more records (there should be 8 consecutive records in all), 1-2-3 bleeps. You can peruse through the chosen records backwards by pressing the up arrow key. Again, if there are no more records that match the chosen criteria, 1-2-3 bleeps when the up arrow key is pressed.

Extracting Records:
The /Data, Query, Extract command copies records that match the chosen criteria from the database to the output range of the worksheet, while the /Data, Query, Unique command does the same thing, but does not copy repeated records. However, before selecting either of these commands, you must use the /Data, Query, Output command to specify the output range into which data is to be copied.

It is imperative that the area below the output range is sufficiently long to accommodate all the extracted records. In our example, as we have chosen the output area to be in a part of the worksheet which has nothing below it, we can specify the output range as K12..S12. Specifying the output range by only the row of field names causes the entire area under these field names to be cleared before the extracted records are copied into the output range. So, beware! If an output range of more than one row is specified, 1-2-3 does not erase the contents of the worksheet below the output range, but if such a multiple-row output range is not large enough to contain all the records that meet the criteria, an error message will be displayed.

The criteria we used previously with the /**Data, Query, Find** command were such that 8 records were found, one of which referred to a customer who had already paid the relevant invoice. To eliminate this customer, add into the criteria selection the entry ~Y in cell O5 and use the /**Data, Query, Extract** command to extract the following records.

```
Q5: (T) [W6] +G5>=80#AND#+G5<330                                    READY

            K              L              M     N      O   P    Q
2  CRITERIA RANGE
3
4          NAME          DETAILS         No   ISSUED  Y/N OVER RANGE
5                                                      ~Y       +G5>=
6
7
8
9
10 OUTPUT RANGE
11
12         NAME          DETAILS         No   ISSUED  Y/N OVER RANGE
13 BARROWS Associates Tunnel Design Tests 9003 17/5/90  N   254   90
14 STONEAGE Ltd       Carbon Dating Tests 9004 29/5/90  N   242  120
15 PARKWAY Gravel     Material Size Tests 9005 14/6/90  N   226  150
16 WESTWOOD Ltd       Load Bearing Tests  9006 27/6/90  N   213  180
17 GLOWORM Ltd        Luminescence Tests  9007  7/7/90  N   203  210
18 WORMGLAZE Ltd      Heat Transfer Tests 9009 16/8/90  N   163  270
19 EALING Engines Dgn Vibration Tests     9010  2/9/90  N   146  300
20
21
INVOICE4.WK1                                          NUM
```

When the /**Data, Query, Extract** command is being executed, the mode indicator changes to MENU, and with Release 2.2 or 2.3 the 'Query Settings' screen or dialogue box is also displayed. After the records have been copied into the output range, selecting **Quit** causes 1-2-3 to return to the READY mode.

7. USING MACROS

A macro is a set of instructions made up of a sequence of key-strokes and commands that you would normally have typed onto the keyboard, but which you type instead into your worksheet as cell entries. After entering and naming a macro it can be invoked by simply typing its name. Thus, a macro is a list of commands which is used to perform a complete task and is used whenever we wish to save time in performing repetitive commands or make a worksheet easier to use.

Creating a Simple Macro

We will now use the worksheet saved under PROJECT3 (see the beginning of Chapter 3) to show how we can add macros to it, to perform 'what-if' type of projections by, say, increasing the 'Wages' bill by 15%. If you haven't saved PROJECT3 on disc, it will be necessary for you to enter the information shown below into 1-2-3 so that you can benefit from what is to be introduced at this point. Having done this, save it under PROJECT3.

If you have saved PROJECT3, then enter 1-2-3 and when the mode indicator reads READY, use the **/File, Retrieve** command to load the file. What should appear on screen is shown below.

```
A1: 'PROJECT ANALYSIS: ADEPT CONSULTANTS LTD                         READY

         A         B         C         D         E         F         G
1    PROJECT ANALYSIS: ADEPT CONSULTANTS LTD
2
3              Jan       Feb       Mar    1st Quart   Average
4    ========================================================
5    Consult: £14,000   £15,000   £16,000   £45,000   £15,000.00
6
7    Costs:
8    Wages       2000      3000      4000      9000     3000.00
9    Travel       400       500       600      1500      500.00
10   Rent         300       300       300       900      300.00
11   Heat/Lght    150       200       150       500      166.67
12   Phone/Fax    250       300       350       900      300.00
13   Adverts     1100      1200      1300      3600     1200.00
14   --------------------------------------------------------
15   Tot Cost:   4200      5500      6700     16400     5466.67
16   ========================================================
17   Profit:     9800      9500      9300     28600     9533.33
18   ========================================================
19   Cumulat:    9800     19300     28600
20
PROJECT3.WK1                                                          NUM
```

105

What we would like to do now is to edit the entries under 'Wages' so that this part of the costs can be increased by 15%. One way of doing this would be to multiply the contents of each cell containing the wages value by 1.15. To do this, we would start by highlighting cell B8 then pressing EDIT (**F2**) to allow us to edit the value in it by adding to the entry '*1.15' which has the effect of multiplying the contents of the cell by 1.15 which would increase its contents by 15%. We would then press <Enter>, press the <Right> arrow key to move to cell C8 and repeat the whole procedure. The exact steps, after highlighting cell B8, are:

Manual Procedure	*Equivalent Macro Steps*
Press F2 to edit cell	EDIT}
Type	*1.15*1.15
Press <Enter>	~
Press <Right> arrow	{RIGHT}

Macros must be entered in an empty part of the worksheet in columnar fashion. Each command could be entered in a different row cell of that column, but since a number of commands can be combined - provided the entry is less than 240 characters long - we choose to do just that by typing in cell H10 the combined macro commands

{EDIT}*1.15~{RIGHT}

and since each of the three months are to be changed, we replicate this entry using the /**Copy** command to the two rows immediately below H10.

Having entered this simple macro, we need to name it. To do this, highlight cell H10 and then use the /**Range, Name, Create** command. At this point you will be asked to enter the macro name which must be composed of a backslash (\) followed by a single character (in Release 2.2 you can name a macro with names up to 15 characters long, if you so wish). In our case, we choose to call this macro **P** (for percent). Thus, type

P	to name the macro
<Enter>	to enter name
<Arrows>	to highlight range of macro (H10..H12)
<Enter>	to confirm range

106

It is also a good idea to name your macro on the worksheet itself so that you can remember its name later. To do this, move the highlighted bar to the cell immediately to the left of the first macro entry and type **\P**.

Before executing any macro, save your worksheet, in this case under the filename MACRO1. This is a simple precaution, because should things go wrong and your macro does unpredictable things to your worksheet, it will be easier to reload the worksheet and edit the incorrect macro than it would be to also have to correct the original worksheet!

To allow viewing of as much of the macro as possible, we have reduced the width of column G to 5 characters. Your screen should now display the following information:

```
G10: [W5] '\P                                                          READY

        B        C        D        E        F        G    H        I
1  NALYSIS: ADEPT CONSULTANTS LTD
2
3     Jan      Feb      Mar    1st Quart   Average
4  ===============================================================
5   £14,000  £15,000  £16,000  £45,000  £15,000.00
6  ===============================================================
7
8      2000     3000     4000     9000     3000.00
9       400      500      600     1500      500.00
10      300      300      300      900      300.00  \P  {EDIT}*1.15~{RIGHT}
11      150      200      150      500      166.67      {EDIT}*1.15~{RIGHT}
12      250      300      350      900      300.00      {EDIT}*1.15~{RIGHT}
13     1100     1200     1300     3600     1200.00
14  ---------------------------------------------------------------
15     4200     5500     6700    16400     5466.67
16  ===============================================================
17     9800     9500     9300    28600     9533.33
18  ===============================================================
19     9800    19300    28600
20  ===============================================================
MACRO1.WK1                                                            NUM
```

To use this macro, highlight the first cell to be updated (in this case B8), press Alt+P - in Releases 2.2 & 2.3 you can also press RUN (Alt+**F3**) and select the name of the macro you want to run from the menu of named ranges. Watch the changes that take place in cell range B8..D8 as a result of the three line macro (an empty row signifies the end of a macro), and beyond to F8, since the contents of cells E8 and F8 depend on the contents of cells B8..D8.

We could use the same macro to increase the other costs by a different percentage, by editing it, but this would be rather an inefficient way of doing it. A better method is to allocate a cell for the % increase, say cell H7, and edit the macro so that reference to that cell is made in absolute terms. For example, in cell G7, type

Incr=

and in cell H7 type the actual % increase (in the previous case this would have been 1.15). Finally, edit the macro to:

{EDIT}*$H$7~{RIGHT}

copy it to the next two consecutive rows, and change the formulae that appear in range B8..D8 (as a result of running the macro) to values, with the use of the /**Range, Value** command. Use the arrow keys to highlight the range to copy from (in this case, B8..D13). On pressing <Enter> you will be asked for the range to copy to (in this case, B8..D13). This is imperative because any attempt to increase costs of a given range for which this has already been done before, will give wrong results, unless formulae in these ranges have been changed to values.

Finally, highlight cell B8 and run the macro by pressing **Alt+P**. The display will change to:

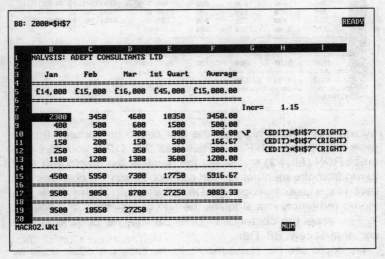

108

Now change the value in cell H7 to 1.20, to attempt to increase the recently increased values in B8..D8 by an additional 20%. You will notice in fact, that as soon as you change the contents of H7, the actual values in cells B8..D8 also change to reflect this new change. This, of course, will inevitably lead to errors, unless you incorporate the command /**Range, Value** within an additional macro which should be executed prior to any attempt in changing the contents of H7. Such a macro could incorporate the following commands:

'/RVB8..D13~B8..D13~

Implement this macro in cell H8 of your current worksheet, name it \V and save the resulting worksheet under the name MACRO2. This macro should be run prior to attempting to change the contents of cell H7. Try it.

Range Names in Macros:
When writing macros it is a good idea to use range names throughout. This allows you to change the location of certain portions of the macro without having to keep track and having to change references to cell addresses; reference to such cells is made by range name rather than discrete cell addressing. For example, the \V macro discussed earlier which had the commands

'/RVB8..D13~B8..D13~

could be rewritten to incorporate the range name 'Costs' as follows:

'/RVCosts~Costs~

where 'Costs' was defined with the use the /**Range, Name, Create** command, as the range name for the cell block B8..D13.

Implement this in your current worksheet, and save the resulting worksheet under the name MACRO2, replacing the previously saved version. Note that we have placed both these macros (macro \P and macro \V) on specific row numbers of column H with a gap between them. This has been done intentionally, so as to allow room for future expansion of this example.

109

What you should have on your screen, is the following display:

```
B8: 2300                                                              READY

      B          C          D          E          F        G     H       I
1  NALYSIS: ADEPT CONSULTANTS LTD
2
3    Jan        Feb        Mar     1st Quart    Average
4  ==================================================================
5  £14,000    £15,000    £16,000    £45,000    £15,000.00
6
7                                                          Incr=    1.15
8    2300       3450       4600      10350     3450.00 \U  /RUCosts~Costs~
9     400        500        600       1500      500.00
10    300        300        300        900      300.00 \P  {EDIT}*$H$7~{RIGHT}
11    150        200        150        500      166.67     {EDIT}*$H$7~{RIGHT}
12    250        300        350        900      300.00     {EDIT}*$H$7~{RIGHT}
13   1100       1200       1300       3600     1200.00
14
15   4500       5950       7300      17750     5916.67
16  ==================================================================
17   9500       9050       8700      27250     9083.33
18  ==================================================================
19   9500      18550      27250
20  ==================================================================
MACRO2.WK1                                                    NUM
```

A final addition to the above macros could be made to allow for
user entry of the 'increment' value from the keyboard, rather
than having to edit cell H7. This can be achieved by the use of
the GETNUMBER macro command, which allows the user to
enter a number which is then inserted into the specified cell in
the worksheet. The general format of this macro command is:

   {GETNUMBER prompt-string,location}

Other available macro commands are listed in Appendix D.

In our particular case, the GETNUMBER command takes the
following form:

   {GETNUMBER "Enter increment ",H7}~

which is typed into cell H9. Don't forget to use the /**Range,
Name, Create** command to re-define macro \V to its new range,
which now should be H8..H12.

Save the resulting worksheet under the filename MACRO3,
before using it. Your screen should now display what is shown
on the next page.

```
        B        C        D        E         F        G    H      I
1  NALYSIS: ADEPT CONSULTANTS LTD
2
3    Jan      Feb      Mar    1st Quart   Average
4  ================================================
5  £14,000  £15,000  £16,000  £45,000  £15,000.00
6  ================================================
7                                               Incr=   1.15
8    2300     3450     4600    10350     3450.00 \U  /RVCosts~Costs~
9     400      500      600     1500      500.00     {GETNUMBER "Enter i
10    300      300      300      900      300.00 \P  {EDIT}*$H$7~{RIGHT}
11    150      200      150      500      166.67     {EDIT}*$H$7~{RIGHT}
12    250      300      350      900      300.00     {EDIT}*$H$7~{RIGHT}
13   1100     1200     1300     3600     1200.00
14
15   4500     5950     7300    17750     5916.67
16  ================================================
17   9500     9050     8700    27250     9083.33
18
19   9500    18550    27250
20  ================================================
MACRO3.WK1                                              NUM
```

As a second example, use the /**Range, Name, Create** command to name the cell block A1..F20 as 'Analysis', then write a macro that will print to the printer the specified range name. Remember that to print the named range manually you would require to issue the following commands:

/	to reveal the menus
P	to select **Print**
P	to select **Printer**
R	to select **Range**

then type the range to be printed and press

<Enter>	to confirm the range selection
A	to select **Align**
G	to select **Go**
Q	to select **Quit**.

Error Checking in Macros:

A macro should be written in such a way as to anticipate any mistakes that might be made by the user. This requires error checking to be incorporated into it so that it provides for possible re-entry of data, rather than cause abrupt exit from the particular application.

111

With this in mind, the macro below has been added to the file MACRO3, incorporating range names and an error routine, as shown below:

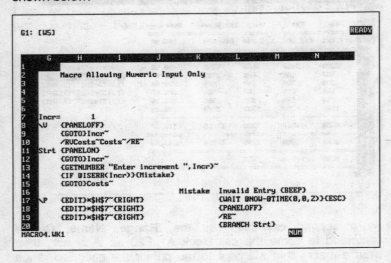

```
G1: [W5]                                                          READY

        G     H        I        J       K       L       M       N
1
2           Macro Allowing Numeric Input Only
3
4
5
6
7   Incr=        1
8   \V   {PANELOFF}
9        {GOTO}Incr~
10       /RUCosts~Costs~/RE~
11  Strt {PANELON}
12       {GOTO}Incr~
13       {GETNUMBER "Enter increment ",Incr}~
14       {IF @ISERR(Incr)}{Mistake}
15       {GOTO}Costs~
16                                   Mistake  Invalid Entry {BEEP}
17  \P   {EDIT}*$H$7~{RIGHT}                  {WAIT @NOW-@TIME(0,0,2)}{ESC}
18       {EDIT}*$H$7~{RIGHT}                  {PANELOFF}
19       {EDIT}*$H$7~{RIGHT}                  /RE~
20                                            {BRANCH Strt}
MACRO4.WK1                                              NUM
```

Make sure that you use the /**Range, Name, Create** command to name the appropriate ranges as follows:

Name	Range
Incr	H7
\V	H8..H15
Strt	H11
Mistake	L16
\P	H17..H19
Costs	B8..D13

The macro checks to see if an error results from a non-numeric entry, and if so, it causes the internal speaker to bleep, and asks for data re-entry. If all is well, the macro causes the cursor to be placed at the beginning of the 'Costs' range so that you can choose which of the various cost categories you would like to update by activating macro \P. Before you run the amended macro, save it under the filename MACRO4.

Macro Learn Mode

Lotus 1-2-3 Release 2.2 & 2.3 provide an easy method of entering repetitive key-stroke type macros into a worksheet - the LEARN mode. Before this feature can be used, a learn range has to be specified in an unused section of the worksheet. To do this, press

/	to reveal the menus
W	to select **Worksheet**
L	to select **Learn**
R	to select **Range**

then specify a single column range that is large enough to store the macro and press <Enter>. Next, press

LEARN   (Alt+**F5**) to turn on the learn feature

and start to perform the series of tasks you want to record. While this feature is activated, the LEARN indicator is displayed at the bottom of your worksheet. After you have finished, press

LEARN   (Alt+**F5**) to toggle off the learn feature

If you look at the learn range now, you will see all the instructions for a macro already typed out. Now name and then run your macro in the usual way. If you want to include another macro in the one you are recording, then enter its range name in braces { }.

As an exercise, use the LEARN mode to create another macro in the MACRO4 file, which can save your worksheet. Compare the result with your manually generated one.

Macro Keys

Most key-strokes can be entered in a macro by typing the appropriate key. All the special macro keys must be typed as shown in the list below. In addition all special keys (with the exception of the <Enter> key symbol) must be enclosed in braces. You can use upper- or lower-case letters when entering the special key names.

Macro Key	Description
~	Enter key
{~}	Tilde appears as ~

113

{{ } and { }}	Braces appear as { and }
{ABS}	ABS (F4); cycles a cell address through relative, absolute, and mixed in POINT and EDIT modes
{APP1}	APP1 (Alt+F7) key
{APP2}	APP2 (Alt+F8) key
{APP3}	APP3 (Alt+F9) key
{APP4}	APP4 (Alt+F10) key
{BIGLEFT}	Move left one screen
{BIGRIGHT}	Move right one screen
{BS}	BkSp; backspace key, erases character to left of cursor. If a range is selected, erases current range
{CALC}	CALC (F9); recalculate formulae in READY mode or converts a formula into its current value in VALUE and EDIT modes
{DEL}	Del; delete key, used in EDIT mode only
{DOWN}	Down arrow key
{EDIT}	EDIT (F2); places highlighted entry on the control panel for editing
{END}	End key
{ESC}	Esc key
{GOTO}	GOTO (F5); moves cell pointer to specified cell
{GRAPH}	GRAPH (F10); view graph most currently specified
{HELP}	This is new to Release 2.2 & 2.3. It produces the same effect as pressing HELP (F1) so that by capturing the key-stroke in a {GET} command, the user is allowed to access the Help screens written for the particular macro.
{HOME}	Home key
{INS}	Ins (insert) key
{LEFT}	Left arrow key
{MENU}	Brings up the 1-2-3 main command menu; the same effect as using the slash (/) or less-than (<) key
{NAME}	NAME (F3); produces a menu of the current range names in POINT mode

{PGDN}	PgDn key
{PGUP}	PgUp key
{QUERY}	QUERY (F7); repeats the last /**Data Query** command
{RIGHT}	Right arrow key
{TABLE}	TABLE (F8); repeats the last /**Data Table** command
{UP}	Up arrow key
{WINDOW}	WINDOW (F6); switches pointer between the two windows when there is a split screen. In Releases 2.2 & 2.3 it can be used to turn on and off the display of settings sheets.

To specify two or more consecutive uses of the same key, use a repetition factor within the braces. For example,

{RIGHT 2} causes the cell pointer to move right twice.

Debugging a Macro

Writing macros can lead to mistakes which you must find and correct. To help you with this task, 1-2-3 provides the STEP mode which allows you to check the execution of your macro step by step. Using this technique, you can see exactly what the macro is doing and where it is going wrong.

To invoke the STEP mode, press the STEP (Alt+**F2**) key. The status indicator at the lower right corner of the worksheet will display the word STEP, and invoking a macro after that, causes its execution to be paused after processing each of its key-strokes.

In Release 2.2 & 2.3, the STEP mode has been enhanced to make it easier to locate errors in a macro. Each time you press a key to execute another macro instruction, 1-2-3 replaces the STEP indicator with the cell address of the cell that contains the macro instruction being executed and the contents of that cell. The current macro instruction (the one to be executed next) is highlighted.

In earlier releases of 1-2-3, when a macro is invoked, the status indicator changes to SST which stands for 'single step'. Pressing any key causes the execution of the next key-stroke in the macro. When the end of the macro is reached, the status indicator changes from SST back to STEP.

Finally, when all the macro commands have been executed, 1-2-3 displays the STEP indicator to remind you that you are still in single step mode. If you press the STEP (Alt+**F2**) key again, the status indicator disappears and any macros you may invoke after that will execute normally.

* * *

Lotus 1-2-3 has many more commands and functions which can be used to build and run your applications in special ways. What this book has tried to do is to introduce you to the overall subject and give the beginner a solid foundation on which to build future knowledge.

* * *

APPENDIX A - INDICATORS

Indicators are highlighted words that appear either in the top right-hand corner of 1-2-3's control panel, or at the bottom of the screen, There are two types of indicators: Mode and Status. The Allways add-in and Wysiwyg module indicators are mostly the same as those used in 1-2-3. Additional ones, specific to Allways or Wysiwyg only, are shown below with a superscripted A ([A]) or W ([W]) after their name, respectively.

Mode Indicators:
Mode indicators appear during every operation of 1-2-3 at the top right-hand corner of the screen. They inform the user of the current state or condition of 1-2-3's operation. The table below lists all the mode indicators with their associated description. The macro command {INDICATE} creates special indicators which are displayed in the same way.

Indicator	Description
ALLWAYS[A]	Allways is ready for you to select a command
EDIT	The current entry is being edited or needs to be edited
ERROR	An error has occurred. Press HELP (**F1**) to display a help screen, or <Esc> to clear it
FILES	A list of files is being displayed
FIND	A /**Data, Query, Find** operation is in progress
FRMT	A format line is being edited during a /**Data, Parse** operation
HELP	The help facility has been invoked
LABEL	A label is being entered
MENU	A command menu is being displayed
NAMES	A menu of existing range, graph, print setting, or @function names is being displayed
POINT	The cell pointer is pointing to a cell or a range of cells
READY	1-2-3 is ready to receive data or a command
STAT	A status screen is being displayed
VALUE	A number or formula is being entered
WAIT	A command or process is being executed
WARN[A]	Allways is displaying a warning message
WYSIWYG[W]	The Wysiwyg menu has been activated.

Status Indicators:

Status indicators appear on the bottom status line of the screen and inform the user of the status of the program or of a key. For example, CALC indicates that the worksheet's formulae need to be recalculated, while CAPS indicates that the <Caps Lock> key is on. The table below lists all the status indicators and gives their description.

Indicator	Description
ANC^	Allways has detected that you have anchored the cell pointer to highlight a range before selecting a command
CALC	The worksheet's formulae need to be recalculated; press the CALC key (**F9**).
CAPS	The <Caps Lock> key is on
CIRC	The worksheet contains a formula that refers to itself (occurs only when the recalculation order is 'Natural', which is the default state). To locate the formula use the **/Worksheet, Status** command
CMD	Program is pausing during a macro execution
END	The <End> key has been pressed
MEM	Less than 4KB of memory is available
LEARN	The LEARN (Alt+**F5**) key has been pressed to turn on the learn feature and 1-2-3 is recording your key-strokes
NUM	The <Num Lock> key is on
OVR	The overstrike mode is on; press the <Ins> key to return to INSERT mode
RO	The status of the current file is read-only
SCROLL	The <Scroll Lock> key is on
SST	A macro currently being run in single-step mode is waiting for user input
STEP	The single-step mode has been activated by pressing the STEP (Alt+**F2**) key
UNDO	The UNDO (Alt+**F4**) key has been pressed to cancel any changes made since 1-2-3 was last in READY mode.

118

APPENDIX B - @FUNCTIONS

Lotus 1-2-3's @functions are built-in formulae that perform specialised calculations. Their general format is:

@name(arg1,arg2,...)

where 'name' is the function name, and 'arg1', 'arg2', etc., are the arguments required for the evaluation of the function. Arguments must appear in a parenthesized list as shown above and their exact number depends on the function being used. However, there are seven functions that do not require arguments and are used without parentheses. These are: @ERR, @FALSE, @NA, @NOW, @PI, @RAND, and @TRUE.

There are four types of arguments used with @functions: numeric values, range values, string values and conditions, the type used being dependent on the type of function. Numeric value arguments can be entered either directly as numbers, as a cell address, a cell range name or as a formula. Range value arguments can be entered either as a range address or a range name, while string value arguments can be entered as an actual value (a string in double quotes), as a cell address, as a cell name or a formula. Condition arguments would normally use logical operators or refer to an address containing a logic formula.

Types of Functions
There are several types of functions, such as mathematical, logical, financial, statistical, string, date and time, special, and database. Each type requires its own number and type of arguments. These are listed below under the various function categories.

Mathematical Functions:
Mathematical functions evaluate a result using numeric arguments. The various functions and their meanings are as follows:

Function	Description
@ABS(X)	Returns the absolute value of X
@ACOS(X)	Returns the angle in radians, whose cosine is X (arc cosine of X)

@ASIN(X)	Returns the angle in radians, whose sine is X (arc sine of X)
@ATAN(X)	Returns the angle in radians, between $\pi/2$ and $-\pi/2$, whose tangent is X (arc tangent of X - 2 quadrant)
@ATAN2(X,Y)	Returns the angle in radians, between π and $-\pi$, whose tangent is Y/X (arc tan of Y/X - 4 quadrant)
@COS(X)	Returns the cosine of angle X (X must be in radians)
@EXP(X)	Raises e to the power of X
@INT(X)	Returns the integer part of X
@LN(X)	Returns the natural logarithm (base e) of X
@LOG(X)	Returns logarithm (base 10) of X
@MOD(X,Y)	Returns the remainder of X/Y
@PI	Returns the value of π (3.1415926)
@RAND	Returns a random number between 0 and 1
@ROUND(X,N)	Returns the value of X rounded to N places
@SIN(x)	Returns the sine of angle X (X must be in radians)
@SQRT(X)	Returns the square root of X
@TAN(X)	Returns the tangent of angle X (X must be in radians).

Logical Functions:

Logical functions produce a value based on the result of a conditional statement, using numeric arguments. The various functions and their meanings are as follows:

Function	Description
@FALSE	Returns the logical value 0
@IF(Cr,X,Y)	Returns the value X if Cr is TRUE and Y if Cr is FALSE
@ISAAF(Name)	Returns 1 (TRUE) if Name is a defined add-in @function, else returns 0 (FALSE)
@ISAPP(Name)	Returns 1 (TRUE) if Name is a currently attached add-in, else returns 0 (FALSE)

@ISERR(X)	Returns 1 (TRUE) if X contains ERR, else returns 0 (FALSE)
@ISNA(X)	Returns 1 (TRUE) if X contains NA, else returns 0 (FALSE)
@ISNUMBER(X)	Returns 1 (TRUE) if X contains a numeric value, else returns 0 (FALSE)
@ISSTRING(X)	Returns 1 (TRUE) if X contains a string value, else returns 0 (FALSE)
@TRUE	Returns the logical value 1.

Financial Functions:

Financial functions evaluate loans, annuities, depreciation and cash flows over a period of time, using numeric arguments. The various functions and their meanings are as follows:

Function	Description
@CTERM(Rt,Fv,Pv)	Returns the number of compounding periods for an investment of present value Pv, to grow to a future value Fv, at a fixed interest rate Rt
@DDB(Ct,Sg,Lf,Pd)	Returns the double-declining depreciation allowance of an asset, with original cost Ct, predicted salvage value Sg, life Lf, and period Pd
@FV(Pt,Rt,Tm)	Returns the future value of a series of equal payments, each of equal amount Pt, earning a periodic interest rate Rt, over a number of payment periods in term Tm
@IRR(Gs,Rg)	Returns the internal rate of return of the series of cash flows in a range Rg, based on the approximate percentage guess Gs
@NPV(Rt,Rg)	Returns the net present value of the series of future cash flows in range Rg, discounted at a periodic interest rate Rt

@PMT(Pl,Rt,Tm)	Returns the amount of the periodic payment needed to pay off the principal Pl, at a periodic interest rate Rt, over the number of payment periods in term Tm
@PV(Pt,Rt,Tm)	Returns the present value of a series of payments, each of equal amount Pt, discounted at a periodic interest rate Rt, over a number of payment periods in term Tm
@RATE(Fv,Pv,Tm)	Returns the periodic interest rate necessary for a present value Pv to grow to a future value Fv, over the number of compounding periods in term Tm
@SLN(Ct,Sg,Lf)	Returns the straight line depreciation allowance of an asset for one period, given the original cost Ct, predicted salvage value Sg, and the life Lf of the asset
@SYD(Ct,Sg,Lf,Pd)	Returns the sum-of-the-years' digits depreciation allowance of an asset, given the original cost Ct, predicted salvage value Sg, life Lf, and period Pd
@TERM(Pt,Rt,Fv)	Returns the number of payment periods of an investment, with amount of each payment Pt, the periodic interest rate Rt, and the future value of the investment Fv

Statistical Functions:

Statistical functions evaluate lists of values using numeric arguments or cell ranges. The various functions and their meanings are as follows:

Function	Description
@AVG(Rg)	Returns the average of values in range Rg
@COUNT(Rg)	Returns the number of non-blank entries in range Rg

Function	Description
@MAX(Rg)	Returns the maximum value in range Rg
@MIN(Rg)	Returns the minimum value in range Rg
@STD(Rg)	Returns the population standard deviation of values in range Rg
@SUM(Rg)	Returns the sum of values in range Rg
@VAR(Rg)	Returns the population variance of values in range Rg

String Functions:

String functions operate on strings and produce numeric or string values dependent on the function.

Function	Description
@CHAR(X)	Returns the LICS (Lotus International Character Set) character that corresponds to the code number X
@CLEAN(Sg)	Removes control characters from a string
@CODE(Sg)	Returns the LICS code number for the first character in string Sg
@EXACT(Sg1,Sg2)	Returns 1 (TRUE) if strings Sg1 and Sg2 are exactly alike, otherwise 0 (FALSE)
@FIND(Ss,Sg,Sn)	Returns position at which the first occurrence of search string Ss begins in string Sg, starting the search from search number Sn
@LEFT(Sg,N)	Returns the first (leftmost) N characters in string Sg
@LENGTH(Sg)	Returns the number of characters in string Sg
@LOWER(Sg)	Converts all the letters in string Sg to lower-case
@MID(Sg,Sn,N)	Returns N characters from string Sg beginning with the character at Sn
@N(Rg)	Returns the numeric value in the upper left corner cell in range Rg

123

@PROPER(Sg)	Converts all words in string Sg to first letter in uppercase and the rest in lower-case
@REPEAT(Sg,N)	Returns string Sg N times. Unlike the repeating character (\), the output is not limited by the column width
@REPLACE(O,S,N,Ns)	Removes N characters from original string O, starting at character S and then inserts new string Ns in the vacated place
@RIGHT(Sg,N)	Returns the last (rightmost) N characters in string Sg
@S(Rg)	Returns the string value in the upper left corner cell in range Rg
@STING(X,N)	Returns the numeric value X as a string, with N decimal places
@TRIM(Sg)	Returns string Sg with no leading, trailing or consecutive spaces
@UPPER(Sg)	Converts all letters in string Sg to uppercase
@VALUE(Sg)	Returns the numeric value of string Sg.

Date and Time Functions:

Date and time functions generate and use serial numbers to represent dates and times. Each date between 1 January, 1900 and 31 December 2099 has an integer serial number starting with 1 and ending with 73050. Each moment during a day has a decimal serial number starting with 0.000 at midnight and ending with 0.99999 just before the following midnight. Thus the value 0.5 indicates midday. The various functions and their meanings are as follows:

Function	Description
@DATE(Yr,Mh,Dy)	Returns the date number of Yr,Mh,Dy
@DATEVALUE(Ds)	Returns the date number of date string Ds
@DAY(Dn)	Returns the day of the month number (1-31) of date number Dn

@HOUR(Tn)	Returns the hour number (0-23) of time number Tn
@MINUTE(Tn)	Returns the minute number (0-59) of time number Tn
@MONTH(Dn)	Returns the month number (1-12) of date number Dn
@NOW	Returns the serial number for the current date and time
@SECOND(Tn)	Returns the second number (0-59) of time number Tn
@TIME(Hr,Ms,Ss)	Returns the time number of Hr,Ms,Ss
@TIMEVALUE(Ts)	Returns the time number of time string Ts
@YEAR(Dn)	Returns the year number (0-199) of date number Dn.

Special Functions:

Special functions perform a variety of advanced tasks, such as looking up values in a table. The various functions and their meanings are as follows:

Function	Description
@@(Ca)	Returns the contents of the cell referenced by cell address Ca
@CELL(At,Rg)	Returns the code representing the attribute At of range Rg
@CELLPOINTER(At)	Returns the code representing the attribute At of the highlighted cell
@CHOOSE(X,V0,..,Vn)	Returns the Xth value in the list V0,..,Vn
@COLS(Rg)	Returns the number of columns in the range Rg
@ERR	Returns the value ERR
@HLOOKUP(X,Rg,Rn)	Performs a horizontal table look-up by comparing the value X to each cell in the top index row, in range Rg, then moves down the column in which a match is found by the specified row number Rn

@INDEX(Rg,Cn,Rw,[W])	Returns the value of the cell in range Rg at the intersection of column-offset Cn, row-offset Rw and worksheet-offset W; used to refer to a look-up table with relative positions rather than the specified values required by @HLOOKUP and @VLOOKUP
@NA	Returns NA (not available)
@ROWS(Rg)	Counts the rows in range Rg
@VLOOKUP(X,Rg,Cn)	Performs a vertical table look-up by comparing the value X to each cell in the first index column, in range Rg, then moves across the row in which a match is found by the specified column number Cn.

Database Functions:

Database functions perform calculations on a database. The database, called the input range, consists of records, which include fields and field names. A criterion range must be set up to select the records from the database that each function uses. The various functions and their meanings are as follows:

Function	Description
@DAVG(Ip,Os,Cr)	Returns the average of the values in the offset column Os, of the input range Ip that meet the criteria in the criterion range Cr
@DCOUNT(Ip,Os,Cr)	Returns the number of non-blank cells in the offset column Os, of the input range Ip that meet the criteria in the criterion range Cr
@DMAX(Ip,Os,Cr)	Returns the maximum value in the offset column Os, of the input range Ip that meet the criteria in the criterion range Cr
@DMIN(Ip,Os,CR)	Returns the minimum value in the offset column Os, of the input range Ip that meet the criteria in the criterion range Cr

@DSTD(Ip,Os,Cr)	Returns the population standard deviation of the values in the offset column Os, of the input range Ip that meet the criteria in the criterion range Cr
@DSUM(Ip,Os,Cr)	Returns the sum of the values in the offset column Os, of the input range Ip that meet the criteria in the criterion range Cr
@DVAR(Ip,Os,Cr)	Returns the population variance of the values in the offset column Os, of the input range Ip that meet the criteria in the criterion range Cr.

APPENDIX C - MACRO COMMANDS

There are a large number of advanced macro commands available in 1-2-3 each one of which has a specified syntax. This takes one of the following two forms:

{Keyword}
{Keyword arg1,arg2,...,argn}

and must be typed into a macro with the prescribed number of arguments. Uppercase and lower-case letters are equivalent in macro keywords and are, therefore, interchangeable. However, it is a good idea to always use a different case for macro commands from that of range names. In the examples given in this book, all macro commands are entered in uppercase, while range names are entered in lower-case. This makes it easier to distinguish between the two.

Note that incorrect macro commands result in an error when the macro is invoked, and not when the macro command is entered. Also, note that there is an important difference between macros and @functions. If you place your macros in any place other than their own worksheet or file, commands that disrupt the sheet layout, such as /**Move**, /**Worksheet, Insert**, or /**Worksheet, Delete** commands with macros, 1-2-3 does not adjust specified cell address, therefore the macro will nor work correctly.

Some macro commands, such as GETNUMBER, change the contents of cells in the worksheet. However, 1-2-3 may not always update or recalculate the worksheet after each macro command is executed. Normally, the inclusion of a tilde (~), which executes an <Enter> at the end of a command accomplishes this, while others require the inclusion of either the CALC (**F9**) instruction, or the {RECALC} macro command, as the next macro instruction. In the following list, a superscript R (^{R}) against a command indicates that a {RECALC} command must be used, while a superscript tilde (~), indicates that a ~ must be used before the worksheet is updated.

Optional arguments are placed in square brackets ([..]), and advanced macros which are new to Release 2.2 & 2.3 or have been greatly enhanced, are shown with a superscript N (^{N}) against their name.

?	{?} stops macro execution temporarily for keyboard input or to allow you to move the cell pointer
BEEP	{BEEP [Num]} causes the speaker to beep. Num is an optional number from 1 to 4 used for different tones (the default value is 1)
BLANK⁻	{BLANK Loc} erases the contents of a specified cell location given by Loc or a range of cells such as A1..A9
BORDERSOFFᴺ	{BORDERSOFF} turns off display of the worksheet frame; similar to {FRAMEOFF}
BORDERSONᴺ	{BORDERSON} worksheet frame back on; similar to {FRAMEON}
BRANCH	{BRANCH Loc} causes macro execution to branch to a different location
BREAKᴺ	{BREAK} clears the control panel contents and returns 1-2-3 to READY mode
BREAKOFF	{BREAKOFF} disables the <Ctrl+Break> key during macro execution
BREAKON	{BREAKON} enables the <Ctrl+Break> key function
CLOSE	{CLOSE} closes a file that has been opened with the OPEN command
CONTENTSᴿ	{CONTENTS Dest,Sour,[Wdth],[Frmt]} places the contents of Source cell, if a 'string', into Destination cell as a label. If the contents of the Source cell are numeric and the *optional* arguments of Width and Format are different from those of the Source cell, then 1-2-3 takes the number in Source together with specified Width and Format and stores it as a left-aligned label in Destination cell
DEFINEᴿ	{DEFINE Loc1:Type1,Loc2:Type2,.Locn.} specifies Location cells and declares Types of arguments to be passed to a subroutine
DISPATCH	{DISPATCH Loc} branches indirectly to the specified destination, given by Loc

FILESIZE[R]	{FILESIZE Loc} determines the number of bytes in a currently opened file and places it in a specified Location
FOR[R]	{FOR Count,Start,Stop,Step,Startloc} executes repeatedly the macro subroutine that begins at the Start location. Count is a cell in which 1-2-3 holds the current number of repetitions, while Startloc is the first cell, or range name, of the subroutine to be executed
FORBREAK	{FORBREAK} cancels execution of current FOR loop
FRAMEOFF[N]	{FRAMEOFF} turns off the display of the worksheet frame
FRAMEON[N]	{FRAMEON} turns on the display of the worksheet frame
GET[R]	{GET Loc} stops macro execution temporarily and stores a single character you type in a specified cell given by Loc
GETLABEL-	{GETLABEL Prompt,Loc} stops macro execution temporarily, prompts you with Prompt string and stores the characters you type as a label in a specified cell given by Loc
GETNUMBER-	{GETNUMBER Prompt,Loc} stops macro execution temporarily, prompts you with Prompt string and stores the characters you type as a number in a specified cell given by Loc
GETPOS[R]	{GETPOS Loc} determines the current position of the file pointer in an open file and displays it in Loc
GRAPHOFF[N]	{GRAPHOFF} removes a graph displayed by {GRAPHON} and re-displays the worksheet
GRAPHON[N]	{GRAPHON [Na],[Nodis]} displays: with no arguments the current graph, the graph named Na, or no graph display but makes Na current

IF	{IF Cond} executes the command that follows, in the same cell, if Cond is true, else moves control to next line down
INDICATE[N]	{INDICATE [String]} shows String as the mode indicator
LET[R]	{LET Loc,String} stores an entered label or {LET Loc,Num} stores an entered number, in a specified cell given by Loc
LOOK[R]	{LOOK Loc} scans the keyboard for input during macro execution and stores that character in Loc
MENUBRANCH	{MENUBRANCH Loc} stops macro execution to allow selection from a customised menu with user-defined choices. The upper left-corner of the menu is given by Loc
MENUCALL	{MENUCALL Loc} stops macro execution to allow menu selection and executes the corresponding macro as a subroutine. The upper left-corner of the menu is given by Loc
ONERROR[R]	{ONERROR Loc,[Msg]} branches to Loc if an error occurs during macro execution. The error message can be optionally recorded at location Msg
OPEN	{OPEN Filename,Mode} opens the specified file in the current directory for reading or writing. Mode is a single character (R for Read, W for Write, M for Modify, or A for Append) which describes the type of file access
PANELOFF[N]	{PANELOFF [Clear]} freezes the control panel during macro operation. If optional Clear is set, the panel is also cleared
PANELON	{PANELON} enables control panel redrawing
PUT[R]	{PUT Loc,Col,Row,String} puts a string or {PUT Loc,Col,Row,Num} puts a number, in the specified Location within a specified range

QUIT	{QUIT} terminates macro execution and returns control to the keyboard
READ[R]	{READ Bytes,Loc} reads a number of bytes (characters) from a file into a cell specified by Loc
READLN[R]	{READLN Loc} copies a line of characters from the currently open file into the specified location
RECALC	{RECALC Loc,[Condit],[Iternum]} recalculates the formulae in a specified range, row by row. Condit and Iternum are optional arguments; Condit is evaluated after the range Location is calculated and if Condit is FALSE, it calculates the range again; Iternum specifies the number of times the range is calculated
RECALCCOL	{RECALCCOL Loc,[Condit],[Iternum]} Recalculates the formulae in a specified range, column by column under the same conditions as RECALC
RESTART	{RESTART} cancels the subroutine and clears the subroutine stack
RETURN	{RETURN} returns from a subroutine
SETPOS	{SETPOS Pointer} sets the file Pointer in the currently opened file into a new position
subroutine_name	{subroutine_name} calls a subroutine
SYSTEM[N]	{SYSTEM Cmd} halts 1-2-3 session to execute DOS command Cmd, then macro continues
WAIT	{WAIT Timenum} suspends macro execution for a specified time
WINDOWSOFF[N]	{WINDOWSOFF} disables redrawing the display screen during macro execution
WINDOWSON[N]	{WINDOWSON} enables normal screen redrawing
WRITE	{WRITE String} copies String into the open text file
WRITELN	{WRITELN String} adds String, plus a carriage return and line-feed sequence, to the open text file.

INDEX

137

NOTES

NOTES